A FLEA
THE SIZE OF PARIS

A FLEA THE SIZE OF PARIS

The Old French *fatrasies* & *fatras*

Translated by Ted Byrne and Donato Mancini

Black Widow Press is an imprint of Commonwealth Books, Inc., Boston, MA. Distributed to the trade by NBN (National Book Network) throughout North America, Canada, and the U.K. All Black Widow Press books are printed on acid-free paper, and glued into bindings. Black Widow Press and its logo are registered trademarks of Commonwealth Books, Inc.

Joseph S. Phillips and Susan J. Wood, Ph.D., Publishers
www.blackwidowpress.com

Cover Art: Tiziana La Melia. "Arrested Pea." (2018).
Design, Typesetting & Production: Kerrie Kemperman

ISBN-13: 978-1-7338924-3-8

Printed in the United States

10 9 8 7 6 5 4 3 2 1

Table of Contents

Preface

A *Flea the Size of Paris* presents translations of texts from thirteenth and fourteenth century France, the poems known as the *fatrasies* and the *fatras*.

As editor and translator Martijn Rus has said, no poetry of the period goes further along the path of linguistic and formal exploration than the fatrasies and the fatras. The *fatrasiers* (fatras-makers) created something like a "new poetic language," as an alternative to the courtly poetic conventions dominant in their time. These poems are in fact so anomalous, in a sense historically "premature" (Paul Zumthor), that they are often compared with Dada and Surrealism.

The fatrasies have come down in two groups. The earliest is a suite of 11 stanzas by Phillipe de Rémi, the form's inventor, composed sometime around 1250, while Rémi was a knight at the court of the Countess Mahaut, in Arras. The larger group of 55 stanzas was composed in the city of Arras, likely sometime between 1280 and 1300. Written by an anonymous collective of poets, the *Fatrasies d'Arras*, as they are called, are found in only a single manuscript.

Of the 71 surviving fatras, the most important are the 30 collected with the works of a court poet named Watriquet de Couvin. Watriquet wrote his fatras in collaboration with an otherwise unknown *jongleur* (travelling poet-performer) named Raimmondin, and possibly with contributions from their audience. Like the *Fatrasies d'Arras*, the Watriquet-Raimmondin fatras are only found in one manuscript.

Only a little is known about the contemporary reception of the fatras: they were performed for Phillippe VI the King of France, on Easter Sunday in 1329 or 1330. Of the fatrasies' reception even less is known, except that in Arras of the period there were well-established poetry societies and popular poetry competitions, for which the poems may have been written.

Formally, a key link between the two forms is that they are dialogic, joining (at least) two distinct voices or distinct styles within a single stanza.

A fatras begins with a framing couplet, usually written in a courtly poetic register. The couplets may have been borrowed from poems already popular at the time, but few sources have been positively identified. A typical example is: "Gently she comforts me / the one who stole my heart." The framing couplet is stated once. The first line of the framing couplet is then restated, after which follows a 9-line sequence of non-sequiturs, dream-like shifts of scale and person, scatological or blasphemous jokes and slapstick routines. The poem culminates in a restatement of the second line of the framing couplet, now re-encountered in an estranging new light. In composing these pieces, Raimmondin's role may have been to provide the couplet, and perhaps also the rhyme words, as a challenge to Watriquet to invent a fatras on the spot. In the manuscript, the fatras' performance is described as a *desputation* (dispute, or debate), suggesting an adjudicated competition and improvisation.

Fatrasies have the same stanza-form, of 11 lines rhymed: *a a b a a b b a b a b*. Without the device of the framing couplet, the dialogic game is heard in the abrupt change of manner between the first 6 lines and the final 5. The first group, of 5 syllables each, are in an almost nursery-rhyme rhythm. They depict impossible protagonists doing impossible things, matter-of-factly: "A big smoked herring / laid siege to Gisors / from all sides at once." The second group, of 7 syllables each, abruptly breaks this rhythm — as if a music box has burst open. The contrast itself, given the artistic context in which the poems were written, suggests a collage-like, collaborative writing procedure. In writing the fatrasies, one poet may have provided the first 6 lines, and/or the rhyme words, as a challenge to another poet to dream up the rest. Or perhaps each poet, in a round of 11 poets, wrote a single line before passing it on to the next poet to write the next line. The truth may never be known.

For readers today, fatrasies and fatras are a noisy mix of levity and malaise, carnival and apocalypse, sudden death and swarming life. Some critics would domesticate them as prankish "antics" or "nonsense," but these terms misrepresent how the poems actually misbehave. In 1432, the poet Baudet Harenc proposed a better term — the "impossible" — to capture their relentlessly disjunctive, irrational, phantasmic unfolding. Rather than "nonsense," the poems are perhaps "unsense": a kind of ultra-logic of the real, in which clearly expressed, concrete acts and actualities make no (common) sense. As Michèle Gally has said, it is not that the fatrasies *mean too little,* but that they *mean too much.* The fatrasies and fatras test the principles through which language is composed into rational forms. With a tissue of rhyme, assonance and homonyms, they stretch semantic sense to its breaking point, across skeletons of good grammar, neat sentences and short, tidy stanzas. As medievalist Bettina Full writes of the *Fatrasies d'Arras,* these poems capture "the fullness, fleeting and mortal, of all human life."

A Flea the Size of Paris:
The Old French *fatrasies & fatras*

The fatrasie of Philippe de Rémi

Li chan d'une raine
Saine une balaine
Ou fons de la mer
& une seraine
Si emportoit Saine
Deseur Saint Omer
Uns muiau i vint chanter
Sans mot dire a haute alaine
Se ne fust Warnaviler
Noié fuissent en le vaine
D'une teste de sengler

1.1

A tree frog's song
drew blood from a whale
on the ocean floor
while a water nymph
hoisted the Seine
beyond Saint-Omer
A mute arrived singing
wordlessly as loud as he could
If not for Warnavillers
they'd have drowned in the veins
of the head of a wild boar

Li piés d'un sueron
Feri un lÿon
Si k'il le navra
La moule d'un jon
A pris un limon
Ki s'en courecha
Mauvais laron le clama
És vous le bech d'un frion
Qui si bien les desmella
Que la pene d'un oison
Trestout Paris emporta

1.2

An itch-mite's left foot
kicked at a lion
so hard that it hurt
A jester's marrow
grabbed at a lime
who choked up with rage
when a robber arraigned him
But the beak of a greenfinch
so completely undid them
that the fluff of a gosling
hauled all of Paris away

Je vi toute mer
Sur tere assambler
Pour faire .i. tournoi
& pois a piler
Sur .i. chat monter
Firent nostre roi
Atant vint je ne sai quoi
Qui Calais & Saint Omer
Prist & mist en un espoi
Si les a fait reculer
Deseur le Mont Saint Eloi

1.3

I saw the whole sea
gathered on land
to fight a tourney
& a peas porridge
mounted a cat
to become our king
when I-do-not-know-what
took Calais & Saint-Omer
& skewered them on a spit
forcing them into retreat
over Mont-Saint-Éloy

Uns grans herens sors
Eut assis Gisors
D'une part & d'autre
& .ii. homes mors
Vinrent a esfors
Portant une porte
Ne fust une vielle torte
Qui ala criant Ahors
Li cris d'une quaille morte
Les eüst pris a esfors
Desous un capel de fautre

1.4

A big smoked herring
laid siege to Gisors
from all sides at once
& two dead soldiers
doubled its forces
by bringing a door
If not for a stale pastry
who rolled by shouting Begone
the cry of a lifeless quail
would've taken them by force
underneath a felt hat

Li cras d'un poulet
Menja au brouet
Pont & Verberie
Li bés d'un coket
Emportoit sans plet
Toute Normendie
& une pume pourie
Qui a feru d'un maillet
Paris & Romme & Surie
Si en fist un gibelet
Nus n'en menjut qui ne rie

1.5

Some chicken fat
chewed on a stew
of Pont & Verberie
A little cock's beak
met no resistance
& took Normandy
& a rotten apple
who'd smashed with a mallet
Paris & Rome & Syria
cooked them in a fricassee
none could eat without laughing

Uns dés estourdis
Portoit Saint Denis
Parmi Mondidier
Et une pertris
Traïnoit Paris
Deseur Saint Richier
És vous le piét d'un plouvier
Sur le clokier de Saint Lis
Qui si haut prist a crier
Quë il a tous estourdis
Les bourgois de Monpellier

1.6

A mixed-up dice
carried Saint Denis ˙
into Montdidier
A red-legged partridge
dragged all of Paris
over Saint-Riquier
But the foot of a plover
on the Senlis bell tower
started shrieking so loud
it completely shook up
the Montpellier bourgeoisie

Une grant vendoise
Entraïnoit Oise
Deseure un haut mont
& une viés moise
Deseure une toise
Emporta Hautmont
Une espane de roönt
.XL. muis de blé poise
Sur le castel de Clermont
Si c'une flestre jorroise
En söoula tout le mont

1.7

A giant catfish
lured the Oise
onto a mountaintop
& a herring-barrel
more than six feet tall
hauled away Hautmont
Up on Clermont castle
a heap of coarse wool shares out
forty bushels of barley
while one dried prune from Jouarre
gets the whole world sloshed

Quatorze viés frains
Aporterent rains
Pour faire un estour
Encontre .ii. nains
Qui eurent es mains
La bouce d'un four
Si en eurent le millour
Pour çou que carbons estains
Leur geterent tout entour
Si k'il eurent ars les mains
Sur le pumel d'une tour

1.8

Fourteen old bridles
carried big branches
just to do battle
against two dwarves
who held in their hands
the mouth of a forge
But they got the upper hand
when they strewed all around them
half-burnt lumps of charcoal
& so scorched all their fingers
on a gate-tower's pommel

Li chiés d'une trelle
Par nuit se resvelle
Pour pestrir pastés
Et une corneille
Prist une corbelle
Ce fu foletés
Car dis et nuef vaissiaus d'és
Coururent a la mervelle
Ja i eüst cox donnés
Quant une chaloreille
D'un baston les a sevrés

1.9

A ruddy fish head
got up in the night
to knead some dough
& then a crow
stole a bread basket
Everything went crazy
because nineteen beehives
rushed in to see this wonder
They'd have all come to blows
but just then a *chaloreille*
drove them apart with a stick

Une viés kemise
Eut s'entente mise
A savoir plaidier
& une cerise
S'est devant li mise
Pour li laidengier
Ne fust une viés cuillier
Qui s'alaine avoit reprise
S'i aportoit un vivier
Toute l'iauwe de Tamise
Fust entree en un panier

1.10

A balding hair-shirt
got into his head
to take up the law
until a cherry
got up in his face
with injurious torts
If not for an old spoon
who'd started to breathe again
& brought along a fishpond
all the water of the Thames
would've debouched in a sieve

Gornais & Ressons
Vinrent a Soissons
Prendre Boulenois
& troi mort taöns
Parmi .iii. flaöns
Mengierent François
Atant i vint Aucerrois
Acourant en .ii. poçons
Si que Chaälons & Blois
S'enfuïrent dusk'a Mons
En Henau par Orelois

1.11

Gournay & Ressons
both came to Soissons
to capture Boulogne
& three dead horseflies
ate up all the French
in three anchovy flans
Auxerrois then ran up
a clay pot on each foot
chasing Châlons & Blois
to Mons in Hainaut
by way of Orléans

The fatrasies of Arras

Jaler sans froidure
Prestoit a usure
Auques por noient
Nule creature
Metoit em presure
Safirs D'Orïant
Biau tans de pluie & de vent
& cler jor par nuit oscure
Firent .i. tornoyement
Sor plain poing de neste ordure
Fondoient coyvre a Dynant

1.1 (1)

The midsummer frost
lent out at high cost
a little for naught
Only one creature
set eastern sapphires
in bezels of rennet
Good weather of wind & rain
& bright day in darkest night
held a jousting tournament
The hardest copper is forged
with a fistful of clean shit

Fourmage de laine
Porte une semaine
A la Saint Remi
& une quintaine
Couroit parmi Saine
Sor pet et demi
Li siecles parti par mi
.I. suirons sainiez de vaine
Leur dit Par l'ame de mi
J'ai repost .i. mui d'avaine
Dedenz le cul d'un fremi

1.2 (2)

A cheese wheel of wool
hauled seven days
to Saint-Rémy fair
& a jousting dummy
sailed over the Seine
on a fart & a half
Our world is so divided
A hemorrhaging bedbug
said to them By my soul
I rammed a hogshead of oats
into the ass of an ant

Uns giex de nipole
Chante une jaiole
De loial amour
.I. chastiaus qui vole
D'une poire mole
Recoussoit .i. four
Ja cheïssent de lor tour
Ne fust une palevole
Qui s'arma devant le jour
Por le gieu de la grimole
Qui minoit la maistre tour

1.3 (3)

A backgammon set
sings a jail song
of statutory love
A castle on wings
sews up an oven
with a quiet fart
Yet they'd botch their attack
if not for a blade of straw
up before sunrise & armed
to undermine the bastion
in a furious staring-match

Andoille de voirre
Aprestoit son oyrre
Por aler nuleu
.I. Flamens d'Auçuerre
Vessoit por miex poirre
De latin en grieu
& uns pez fait en ebrieu
I faisoit hanas de Juerre
Molt em faisoit grant aleu
Qant .i. petiz faiz de fuerre
Commença .i. noviau geu

1.4 (4)

A sausage of glass
was packing its bags
for a trip to nowhere
A Flemish Frenchman
swelled up to belch better
his Latin in Greek
A fart spoken in Hebrew
drew a forty-ounce pint
& it cost him dearly
when a little straw man
started the game anew

Dui rat userier
Voloient songier
Por faire .i. descort
.III. faucons lanier
On fait plain panier
Des Vers de la Mort
.I. muiaus dit qu'il ont tort
Por l'ombre d'un viez cuvier
Qui por miex villier s'endort
Qui cria Alez lacier
Por tornoier sanz acort

1.5 (5)

Two usurious rats
hoped that in dreaming
they'd write a descort
Three timid falcons
filled a breadbasket
with worm-eaten dirges
A mute declared that they'd erred
since the shade of an old tub
asleep to stay more awake
shouted Go ahead gear-up
for a contest without end

Formaige de grue
Par nuit esternue
Sor l'abai d'un chien
.I. coutiaus maçue
Saut et si le hue
Si ne li dit rien
.I. escharbos lit dit bien
Qant li dos d'une sansue
Qui confessoit .i. mairien
Ja chie tant l'ont batue
Dient cil fusicien

1.6 (6)

An idiot cheese
sneezes at night
whenever dogs bark
A razor-sharp club
jumps up & berates it
but says not a word
A dung-beetle gave blessing
when a leech's backside
on hearing a joist confess
was smacked so hard that it shat
just as the doctors prescribe

En l'angle d'un con
La vi .i. taisson
Qui tissoit orfrois
& .i. chapperon
Parmi Monloön
Menoit Vermendois
Je lor dis en escoçois
Des coilles d'un papillon
Porroit on faire crazpois
& dou vit d'un limeçon
Faire chastiax & berfrois

1.7 (7)

Deep down in a cunt
I saw a badger
weaving gold brocades
& a monk's cowl
drove Vermandois
right across Laon
I asked them in Scottish
Could we lard our baked beans
with a butterfly's balls
build castles & belfries
with the penis of a snail

Uns mortiers de plume
But toute l'escume
Qui estoit en mer
Ne mais une enclume
Qui molt iert enfrume
Si l'en va blamer
.I. chas emprist a plorer
Si que la mer en alume
.I. juedi aprés souper
La convint il une plume
.IIII. truies espouser

1.8 (8)

A mortar of down
would've drunk all the spume
that's found in the sea
if not for an anvil
who makes a dour face
when you insult it
A cat sobbed so grievously
he set the sea on fire
One Thursday after supper
he obliged a feather
to wed a foursome of sows

Je vi une tour
Qui a .i. seul tour
Vola duqu'a nues
Si vi demi jour
Entrer en .i. four
Aprés .iiii. grues
Se ne fussent .ii. maçues
Qui d'une arbaleste a tour
Orent .ii. nonnains foutues
Mortes fussent sanz retour
.IIII. cotes descousues

1.9 (9)

I saw a tower
with one nimble spin
fly up to the clouds
I watched a noon hour
follow four cranes
into an oven
If not for two gnarled clubs
shot from a huge arbalest
who knocked up two nuns
four unbuttoned tunics
would be incurably dead

Je vi une crois
Chevauchier Artois
Sor une chaudiere
& une viez sois
Menoit Vermendois
Parmi une pierre
Se ne fust une verriere
.II. lymeçons voire .iii.
De Paris duqu'en Baiviere
Eüssent fait .x. Anglois
Huchier Harpë et Godiere

1.10 (10)

I saw a crucifix
bestraddle Artois
atop a cauldron
while an old hedge row
led the Vermandois
straight through a stone wall
If not for a glass lantern
two turtles or even three
would have made ten Englishmen
shout *Harpë et Godiere*
from Paris to Bavaria

Je vi Saint Quentin
Qui de Saint Aubin
Feri Saint Omer
Arras et Blangi
Derierre Chauni
Lor trossiax porter
.I. surons les voust rober
Se ne fussent .ii. poucin
C'uns Anglois devoit couver
Traïs fust Salahadins
A l'entree de la mer

1.11 (11)

I saw Saint-Quentin
cudgel Saint-Omer
Arras & Blangy
into hauling their trunks
from Saint-Aubin
to the far side of Chauny
A flea wished to rob them
If not for two goslings who
some Anglo was due to brood
Saladin would have fallen
at the brink of the sea

Chates escorchies
Erent enragies
Por peler blans aus
.II. truies noïes
S'en sont couroucies
S'ont pris .ii. pestaus
Se ne fust .i. gris vëaus
.II. suris forspaïsies
Qui venoient de Cytiax
Estoient ja conseillies
De porter Paris a Miax

2.1 (12)

A gang of skinned cats
drove themselves crazy
peeling white garlic
A pair of drowned sows
maddened by this
snatched up two pestles
But for an old grizzled calf
two refugee field mice
from the Abbey of Cîteaux
would've chosen already
to drag Paris to Méaux

Uns viellars mors nez
Qui avoit court nez
Portoit .i. molin
Uns chas bestornés
C'est bien atornés
De .ii. dras de lin
Plain possonnet de saïn
Les eüst touz estonnés
A l'entree d'un jardin
Qant uns ras i a menez
Les pez d'un viez Tartarin

2.2 (13)

A stillborn geezer
with a short sneezer
hefted a windmill
An upside-down cat
wrapped himself neatly
in two linen shrouds
They'd have all been amazed
by a small pot of suet
at the gate of a garden
when a rat spread before them
the farts of an old Tartar

Allie d'estrain
Formage de pain
& feves de pois
& kailleus de grain
& pierres de fain
& Escot françois
.I. chas qui parloit grijois
Emportoit seignor Alain
Dont ce fu trop grans anois
Qant .ii. singe chastelain
Chevauchoient Vermendois

2.3 (14)

Aioli of straw
a cheese made of bread
& beans made of peas
& pebbles of grain
& stones made from hay
& one Gallic Scot
A cat speaking Greekish
took Lord Alain hostage
which became too much trouble
when two castellan monkeys
mounted & rode Vermandois

Uns cendaus de laine
Estoit en grant paine
De corber .i. pois
Por sainier de vaine
Venoit Babilaine
Apenre françois
Encontre vint Vermendois
Qui hanissoit sans alaine
Sor .i. grant cheval d'orfrois
Par .i. jour hors de semaine
S'emfuient .xiiii. mois

2.4 (15)

Some wool taffeta
was taking great pains
to fuck a pea pod
To have her veins bled
Great Babylon came
for lessons in French
Vermandois came to fight
& then silently brayed
on a steed of gold braid
Fourteen months fled away
one non-calendrical day

Moustarde d'anete
Portoit Damïete
Derier Occident
.I. viz de cherete
Batoit l'entrepete
Plain panier de vent
.I. chas qui la lune vent
Saut avant & si culete
.X. fremis en .i. couvent
Si que Paris en volete
D'Acre duqu'en Occident

2.5 (16)

A duckling mustard
dragged Damietta
behind the west wind
A stiff carriage shaft
battered the cervix
of a basket of air
A cat hawking the moon
jumped from ahead & behind
ten ants in a convent
so that Paris fluttered back
from Acre to the Occident

Li sons d'un cornet
Mengoit a l'egret
Le cuer d'un tonnoire
Qant .i. mors bequet
Prist au trebuchet
Le cours d'une estoile
En l'air ot .i. grain de soile
Qant li abais d'un brochet
& li tronçons d'une toile
Ont trové foutant .i. pet
Si li ont coupé l'oreille

2.6 (17)

The sound of a horn
ate with verjuice
a thunderclap's heart
when a dead salmon
caught in a bird-trap
the path of a star
A rye seed was marching on air
when the bark of a pike
& the stump of a hank
found a fart fucking
& chopped off its ear

Crasses pierres moles
Tenoient escoles
Por pés endormir
.II. vielles cytoles
Vuidoient fioles
... mouches vessir
... ai bien ce que je desir
... commencent les quaroles
... avoient bon loisir
... a laus kyrïoles
... venoient de pestrir

2.7 (18)

Some soft fatty stones
offered instruction
to put farts to sleep
Two aging citoles
voided some viols
so flies could break wind
I have just what I want
once the singing begins
those who came to knead dough
have a leisurely time
during lauds & Kyries

Dragons de geline
Devenoit ferine
Por avoir argent
.I. herens se pingne
Por avoir haïne
De dyversses gent
Molt se vivoit bel et gent
Cil qui savoit lor covine
.I. mostiers i vint nagant
Qui avoit moustré s'orine
D'Acre duqu'en Occident

2.8 (19)

A chicken-dragon
turned into flour
to pull down some coin
A kipper combed its hair
to win the hatred
of a wider public
Many who know their own minds
live in style & in comfort
A monastery took a swim
to leave a trail of urine
from Acre to the Occident

Anguiles de terre
Fesoient grant guerre
D'eles comfesser
Ne mais Engleterre
Mengoit Engleterre
Por s'ame sauver
.I. mors hom s'i fist porter
& uns huis qui se deserre
Voloit aler outremer
Atout .i. chapelet d'ierre
Le juedi aprés souper

2.9 (20)

The eels of the land
waged glorious war
to confess their sins
but England was found
eating English soil
to buy back its soul
A corpse had himself brought there
& a self-opening door
wanted to sail overseas
on an ivy rosary
one Thursday after supper

Une palevole
Tornoit une mole
De marbre porfire
& une brifole
Venoit de l'escole
D'un parage lire
.I. chapaus de chaz en mire
Noviax revenus d'escole
Li prist vilonie a dire
La nuit jut avec s'ailole
S'engenra .i. voust de cire
....

Molt en tinrent grant consile
Tuit li gieu de la grimole
Se n'o reson ne parole
Tuit li cors d'un cimentire
Se pristrent a la karole
Chascun set chanter & lire
& harper a la viole

2.10 + 2.11 (21)

A wisp of straw
turned a millstone
of porphyry marble
& a big glutton
arrived from the school
of lineal thought
A cat's cap stared wide-eyed
Just now returning from school
he said some vile things to him
Evening jousted his grandma
& sired a wax effigy
. . . .
Many found wisdom in these
games of taunts & counter-taunts
not without reason or plaint
Every corpse in the graveyard
began to sing & dance a round
They all knew how to sight-read
& play harp on a fiddle

Uns kailleus veluz
Devenoit rendus
Ses pechiez plourant
& uns vieue baüs
Ocist .iiii. dus
Son cors desfendant
Mais mal lor fust convenant
Se ne fust uns eternus
Qu'il .iii. firent en dormant
Qui dit que li rois Artus
Estoit gros de vif emfant

3.1 (22)

A hairy pebble
became a recluse
& wept for his sins
An old locked box
defending his goods
slaughtered four dukes
But they'd have all come to grief
were it not for a sneeze
all three sneezed while asleep
which disclosed that King Arthur
was pregnant with a grown child

Li pez d'un suiron
En son chapperon
Voloit porter Romme
.I. oés de coton
Prist par le menton
Le cri d'un preudomme
Ja le ferist en la somme
La pensee d'un larron
Qant li pepins d'une pomme
C'est escriez a haut ton
Dont viens Ou vas
Huillecomme

3.2 (23)

The fart of a mite
in its little hat
tried to capture Rome
An egg of cotton
grabbed by the chin
a councilor's chagrin
A burglar's idea
would have struck him in the end
when the pip of an apple
cried out in falsetto
Where from Where to
Willkommen

Li ombres d'un oef
Portoit l'an renuef
Sus le fonz d'un pot
.II. viez pingne nuef
Firent .i. estuef
Pour courre le trot
Qant vint au paier l'escot
Je qui omques ne me muef
M'escriai si ne dis mot
Prenez la plume d'un buef
S'en vestez .i. sage sot
Dorenlot va dorenlot
Tex est couz qui n'en set mot

3.3 (24)

The shade of an egg
brought in the new year
in a pot's bottom
Two brand new old combs
played a game of handball
to run at a trot
When it came time to pay up
I who never shuts my mouth
cried out so as to not say
Pluck a feather from an ox
to dress up a wise moron
Dorenlot va dorenlot
only a cuckold won't know

Une viez paele
Touz cex de Broucele
Voloit compissier
& une vïele
Chantoit em fessele
Dou Danoys Ogier
Sor le comble d'un moustier
Vi .i. tonnel qui rapele
Les montes d'un userier
Qant Auçuerres et Rochele
L'empristrent a esmaier

3.4 (25)

An old frying pan
wanted to piss on
everyone in Brussels
Inside a cheese sieve
a viol sang out
of Ogier the Dane
From atop a church tower
I saw a barrel write off
all a usurer's interest
when Auxerre & La Rochelle
were overcome with concern

Estranges privez
Estoit porpensez
De grant courtoisie
En .ii. saz troez
Avoit aportez
Touz cels de Percie
A Paris en Sacalie
La les eüst delivrez
Em plain hanap de boulie
Qant .i. lymeçons armez
Hautement Monjoie escrie

3.5 (26)

An intimate stranger
committed himself
to true courtesy
In two leaky sacks
he transported all
the people of Persia
to Rue Sacalie in Paris
He was about to unload them
into a goblet of porridge
when a heavily-armed snail cried
Monjoie at the top of his lungs

Li piez d'une sele
Chevauche Rochele
De Hui a Dynant
& une paele
Tondoit sa cotele
De Bruges a Gant
.I. molins i vint volant
Qui ot pris une arondele
.I. caillex i vint plorant
& une putain pucele
Delivree d'un tyrant

3.6 (27)

A footstool's leg
rode La Rochelle
from Huy to Dinant
& a cooking-pot
trimmed his short smock
from Bruges to Ghent
A windmill who'd just captured
a lapwing came soaring in
A pebble-bird arrived in tears
with a celibate slut
he'd freed from a tyrant

Uns chevax de cendre
Crioit pois a vendre
D'un pet de suiron
.I. pez ce fist pendre
Por li miex deffendre
Derier .i. luiton
La s'en esmervilla on
'Que tantost vint l'ame prendre
La teste d'un porion
Pour ce qu'il voloit aprendre
De Gerart de Rossillon

3.7 (28)

A horse of ashes
cried Peas for sale
For its own safety
a peace treaty hung itself
behind a sea sprite
from an itch-mite's fart
We were completely amazed
when his soul came right back
to steal the bulb of a leek
because he wanted to read
the epic of *Rousillon*

Uns pez a .ii. cus
S'estoit revestus
Por lirre gramaire
& uns chas cornus
Devenoit reclus
Si vesti la haire
Li pans d'une manche vaire
Lor a dist Traiés ensus
En chantant les faisoit taire
Qant li ombres d'un seüs
I corut ses braies traire

3.8 (29)

A two-asshole fart
put on his vestments
to read a grimoire
A kitten with horns
became a recluse
& donned a hair-shirt
A shred of a patchwork sleeve
said to them Fall back Retreat
By singing he silenced them
when a basset-hound's shadow
ran up to pull down their pants

Uns arbres reöns
Par desus Soissons
Traïnoit la mer
Uns esmerillons
De ces allerons
L'aloit esventer
Ja feïst tout craventer
Se ne fust .i. limeçons
Qui la terre ot a garder
Qui commanda .ii. oisons
.IIII. larrons trainer

3.9 (30)

A circular tree
was lugging the sea
overtop Soissons
A pigeon hawk
was about to fan him
with both of his fins
He would have wrecked everything
were it not for one snail
who had the earth under guard
& commanded two goslings
to drag four crooks through the street

Demi mui d'avaine
Ce sainoit de vaine
Por aqueillir los
Une quarantaine
Grant joie demaine
Par derier son dos
Se ne fust li ris d'un coç
Qu'entre Pentecouste et Braine
Dont la char ronga les os
Pendus fust en la semaine
Te rogamus audi nos

3.10 (31)

Half a ton of oats
cut open its veins
to win accolades
Behind its back
a forty-day fast
was having a feast
If not for a cock's chuckle
between Pentecost & Braine
whose flesh chewed on his bones
he'd have hanged before Friday
Te rogamus audi nos †

† *We beseech Thee, hear us*

Quatre rat a moie
Faisoient monnoie
D'un viez corbillon
.I. moines de croie
Faisoit molt grant joie
De foutre .i. bacon
Entendez a ma raison
Se ne fust La Pommeroie
Qui chevauchoit .i. gojon
Pendus fust par la courroie
Karesmes par .i. coillon

3.11 (32)

Four rats in a haystack
were minting gold coins
from a rusty ploughshare
A monk made of chalk
rose to his glory
fucking a pork hock
Hear my final summation
If not for La Pommeraye
who was riding a gudgeon
Lent would have been strung up
with his money-belt by one ball

Vache de pourcel
Aingnel de vëel
Brebis de malart
Dui lait home bel
& dui sain mesel
Dui saiges sotart

....

Dui emfant nez d'un torel
Qui chantoient de Renart
Seur la pointe d'un coutel
Portoient Chastel Gaillart

4.1 (33)

One baby pig cow
one baby cow lamb
one puddle-duck ewe
two ugly beauties
two healthy lepers
two stupid sages
....
two children born of a bull
singing the *Roman de Renart*
on the point of a dagger
carried off Castle Gaillard

Uns biaus hom sans teste
Menoit molt grant feste
Por mengier cailliaus
Molt est fiere beste
Cil qui l'en arreste
.I. juedy a Miaus
& .iiii. asnesses sanz piax
Demenoient molt grant feste
Por aus tolir lor drapiaus
Illueques chantoit de geste
Une cuve en .ii. tonniaus

4.2 (34)

A handsome headless man
laid on a great feast
just to eat pebbles
It took a proud beast
to call off this show
one Thursday at Méaux
Four skinless donkeys
had the time of their lives
peeling off all their clothes
so a tub on two barrels
could sing songs of their deeds

Rose de vendoise
Sor la riviere d'Oise
Chevauchoit une ais
Molt menoit grant noise
.I. faisiaus d'ardoise
Parmi .i. tarquais
Tuit li herenc de Qualais
Burent plain pot de cervoise
Chiez l'evesque de Biauvais
Qui confessoit une aisele
Des pechiez qu'elle avoit fais

4.3 (35)

A rose of fish-skin
straddled a plank
on the river Oise
A cheese-basket of slate
inside a quiver
made a heap of noise
Every herring in Calais
drank big jugs of small beer
at the Bishop of Beauvais'
who was confessing an armpit
of all the sins it had done

A champ et a vile
Sa quenoille file
Sans piez et sans mains
Molt savoit de guile
Cil qui d'Abevile
Chevauchoit a Rains
.I. grans homs qui estoit nains
Qui amenoit bien .x. mile
De singes touz chapelains
Davinés ou croiz ou pile
Li premiers fu deësrains

4.4 (36)

Through country & town
her distaff spun
with no hands or feet
Whoever would ride
Abbeville to Reims
must know all the tricks
A giant who was a dwarf
herded ten thousand at least
chimpanzees all of them priests
Call it either heads or tails
the first will be last in line

Uns chiens escorchiez
Estoit escourciez
Por mostiers semer
& uns pygnes viez
S'en est courouciez
C'est saillis en mer
Tant empristrent a parler
Gelines a .iiii. piez
Qu'elles pristrent .i. cengler
Firent de plain pot de miés
Illueques l'asne voler

4.5 (37)

A dog who'd been flayed
hiked up his britches
to father a church
at which an old comb
flew into a rage
& leapt in the sea
Some four-footed chickens
got so caught up in gossip
they brought down a razorback
& from a pitcher of mead
made a donkey take flight

Estrons sans ordure
La mer amesure
Com longue ele estoit
& uns oés de bure
Li dit Hure Hure
Qant il l'aperçoit
.I. mors homs qui bien veoit
Dit Violas Bure Bure
.I. chas qui Paris portoit
Y coroit grant aleüre
Pour ce que nus piez n'avoit

4.6 (38)

A shitless turd
measured the ocean
to find out its girth
An egg of butter
as soon as he heard
replied Hurrah Hurrah
A corpse with good eyesight
shouted *Violas Bure Bure*
A cat carrying Paris
ran over in quite a hurry
given that he had no feet

Grant noise faisoient
Dui pet qui metoient
Une suris en sel
Dui four en tomboient
.II. truies chantoient
Parmis .i. tynel
Molt parloient d'un et d'el
.II. suris qui emportoient
Rains et Paris sor .i. pel
Si que forment em plouroient
Pasques derierre Noël

4.7 (39)

As two farts packed
a rat into salt
& made a racket
two ovens fell out
Two sows sang carols
deep in a carafe
Two mice carried overhead
Reims & Paris on a pike
gabbing of this & of that
so much that they made Easter
weep behind Christmas's back

Tripe de moustarde
Se faisoit musarde
Dou poistron s'antain
& uns oés ce farde
Pour ce quë il n'arde
D'un pet de putain
C'est de la Chançon d'Audain
Lors i vint une bystarde
Qui fu commere Bertain
& une truie gaillarde
.I. mostier dedenz son sain

4.8 (40)

Tripes made of mustard
were loafing about
on their aunt's arse
An egg put on rouge
so as to not get burnt
by a prositute's fart
It's all in the *Song of Audain*
Along came a bustard
who was Bertha's godmother
& a strapping young sow
with a church between her tits

Saÿn de marmothe
Chantoit une note
De Mante a Paris
Une saige sote
D'une chappe cote
Li a fait .i. ris
Bien fust chascons d'aus garnis
Ne fust .i. estivaus bote
Qui portoit en .ii. baris
.I. chastel sor une mote
Si les a touz esmaris

4.9 (41)

Some marmoset lard
sang one steady note
from Mantes to Paris
From a trouser-shirt
a cretinous sage
sewed himself a smile
They'd all've been garnished with garlic
if not for a sandal-boot
who carried in two barrels
a castle built on a hill
which left everyone confused

Uns biaüs hom sans teste
Menoit molt grant feste
Por .i. com velut
& une fenestre
A mis hors sa teste
Si vit le fendu
Ja fust grant max avenu
Qant li songes d'une beste
S'escria Hareu le fu
Trestout voloit ardoir l'aitre
Pour ce c'om i ot foutu

4.10 (42)

A handsome headless man
laid on a great feast
for a hairy cunt
Just then a window
stuck out its noggin
& noticed the crack
Bad things were about to happen
when the dream of a donkey
brayed Hey Help Fire Fire
Everyone wants the altar
where we all got fucked to burn

Uns corz sainz de Cille
Fist d'un cuir d'anguille
La lune lever
& une morille
Avoit une fille
Qui portoit la mer
Mort fussent a l'ariver
Se ne fust une faucille
Qui les ala delivrer
Por .i. byreliquoquille
Le juedy au soupper

4.11 (43)

A holy relic
made the full moon rise
out of an eel skin
A putrid cadaver
gave birth to a girl
pregnant with the sea
All were dead on arrival
if not for a sickle blade
who came to deliver them
for a *byreliquoquille*
on Thursday during supper

Bacin chandelier
Furent sommelier
Au roy Dagombert
Bien savoit villier
& lui travillier
Li poitrons Aubert
& li pez sire Gombert
Les ala touz esvillier
Dex vous saut sire Robert
.IIII. sous en .i. denier
Chanta de saint Filebert

5.1 (44)

Candlestick bathtubs
were surrogate sleepers
to King Dagobert
D'Aubert's derrière
knew how to stand watch
& how to torment him
& the fart of Sir Gombert
woke up the whole household
God blast you Sir Robert
Four nickels in a penny
sang songs of Saint Philibert

Hasart de .ix. poinz
Estraint si ses poinz
C'uns bués en sailli
Molt fu or prez poinz
.I. viviers pourpoinz
Quant il li failli
Uns escharbos l'assailli
Qui avoit ces sollers oinz
Tost i fussent malbailli
Se ne fust .i. grans besoinz
Qui venoit devers Mailli

5.2 (45)

A nine-point dice
clenched its fists so tight
an ox leapt out
A needlepoint pond
was pricked with remorse
when it missed its mark
A cockchafer with greased shoes
leapt up & attacked him
They'd all have got a thrashing
if not for an urgent need
sweeping north from Mailly

Une truie enceinte
Parmi une aceinte
Compissoit .i. lievre
Une lamppe estainte
Faisoit sa complainte
Sor plain pot de fievre
Une aloete coviere
Avoit une estille atainte
Sor la keue d'une chievre
Si l'a si dou cul empainte
Que li murs de Paris crieve

5.3 (46)

A keg round with child
fenced-in on all sides
pissed on a hare
A snuffed blubber-lamp
laid charges against
a pot full of flu
A skylark brooding her eggs
brandished a curry-comb
over the tail of a goat
then slapped its ass so hard
the walls of Paris came down

La keue d'un pet
Parmi .i. corbet
Demenoit grant joie
Si vi Mahommet
Sor .i. tonnelet
Faire une viez voie
Saint Quentin Peronne Roie
Mussoient en .i. cornet
Parmi l'ueil d'une lamproie
Qui lor jooit par abbet
D'un oef a boute en corroie

5.4 (47)

The tail of a fart
was getting its kicks
with a crooked saw
watching Mohammad
atop a wine cask
do an old routine
Saint-Quentin & Péronne & Roie
wasted time in a dice-cup
in the eye of a lamprey
who played them all for fools
with an egg in a finger-trap

Anglois de Hollande
Embloient Illande
Por mengier as aus
.I. lymeçons mande
Gent de huppelande
Sor .ii. syminiaus
.I. paniers ce fist chevaus
Qant une mouche truande
Qui fist parler .ii. muiaus
Avoit ja tolu l'offrande
A .ii. abbés de Cytiaus

5.5 (48)

A Dutch Englander
stripped Ireland bare
to eat it with garlic
A snail commanded
people in long gowns
atop two Lenten cakes
A basket became a horse
when a malingering fly
restored speech to two mutes
who'd accepted offerings
from two abbots of Cîteaux

Chançons em poree
Orent acoree
Une viez cité
Une demouree
Embla la Mouree
Par humilité
Qui veïst fragilité
Qui ot sa tonne afforee
Enz ou cul de venité
Cil qui font blanc por mouree
C'en sont molt bien aquité

5.6 (49)

Songs in leek pottage
had pulled out the guts
of an ancient city
A lengthy delay
had ravished Morée
with humility
who had seen fragility
hammer its wooden spigot
into vanity's bunghole
Those who mistake white for black
acquitted themselves quite well

Uns saiges sans sens
Sans bouche sans dens
Le siecle menga
& .i. sors herens
Manda les Flamens
Qui les vengera
Mais tout ce ne lor vaura
La plume de .ii. mellens
Qui .iiii. nés affondra
Mais je ne sai que je pens
De murdre les apela

5.7 (50)

A sage without brains
with no mouth or teeth
devoured the world
A pickled herring
marshalled the Flemish
who would avenge them
But all of this wasn't worth
one feather from two rockfish
who capsized four galleys
Yet I don't know that I think
it should be called murder

Flaöns de noient
Ce lui apartient
Qui portoit Champaigne
Molt bien li avient
Mais ne li sovient
D'aler em Bretaigne
.I. chaperons li enseigne
& uns tacons le detient
Qui emportoit Alemaigne
Mais ne sai quoi qu'il devient
Cil a la chiere grifaigne

5.8 (51)

A cake of nothing
is kin to the one
who carried Champagne
Though heaped with rewards
he never once thought
to take Brittany
A hat gave him instructions
& a boot-heel arrested him
for kidnapping Germany
But I don't know what became
of the one with the gryphon face

Uns nis de croyere
Ce devant derierre
Contoit sa raison
Une fort jangliere
Estoit coustumiere
De moustrer son con
.I. fourmaiges de mouton
Aportoit en sa loiere
Le Jour de l'Asencïon
Qui avoit en s'aumoniere
.XL. jours de pardon

5.9 (52)

The nest of a crow
ass-end out front
presented its case
A ruthless gossip
was in the habit
of flaunting her cunt
A wheel of sheep's cheese
carried home in its game-bag
the Day of the Ascension
who had in its coin-purse
forty days of forgiveness

Blanche robe noire
D'un sens sans mimoyre
Faisoit .i. lorain
Li flairs d'une poire
D'un pet de provoire
Lor chantoit d'Audain
Ce fu es prez Saint Germain
C'uns kaillex qui ot la foyre
Ce faisoit cousins Evain
Ez vos sus une papoire
Criant .i. cortois vilain
Chiens ne m'abaie
Mie tien de mon pain

5.10 (53)

A white black dress
of vaporous insight
was used as a rein
The pear-like bouquet
of a curate's fart
sang songs of Audain
In the fields of Saint-Germain
a stone with diarrhea
who thought he was Eve's cousin
heard a courtly peasant shout
inside a wicker dragon
Dogs please don't bark at me
take a piece of my bread

Uns ours emplumés
Fist semer uns blés
De Douvre a Wissent
Uns oingnons pelez
Estoit aprestés
De chanter devant
Qant sor .i. rouge olifant
Vint uns limeçons armés
Qui lor aloit escriant
Fil a putain sa venez
Je versefie en dormant

5.11 (54)

A feathered bear
sowed a field of wheat
from Dover to Calais
A peeled onion
was getting warmed up
to lead with a song
when atop a red elephant
came a heavily-armed snail
who ran around shouting
Son of a bitch Bring it on
I write poems in my sleep

Anguiles de terre
Faisoient grant guerre
D'eles comfesser
Ne mais Engleterre
Mengoit une pierre
Por s'ame sauver
.I. mors hom s'i fist porter
& uns huis qui se deserre
Voloit aler outremer
Atout .i. chapelet d'ierre
Le juedy apres souper

5.11b (55)

The eels of the land
waged glorious war
to confess their sins
but England was found
devouring a stone
to buy back its soul
A corpse had himself brought there
& a self-opening door
wanted to sail overseas
on an ivy rosary
one Thursday after supper

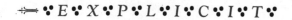

Cy fenissent les fatrasies d'Arras

The grafted fatras by Watriquet de Couvin & Raimmondin

Ci commencent li fastras de quoi
Raimmondin & Watriquet desputerent
le jour de Pasques devant le roy
Phelippe de France

Aprenez a mengier joute
Vous qui ne goustés de pois

Aprenez a mengier joute
Qu'en son cul ne vous engloute
La marrastre des .iii. rois
Qui a l'entrepete route
Pour une culaine goute
Qui la tient ou trou brenois
Si n'i puet aidier tremois
Ne nulle riens c'on i boute
Qu'adés ne soille li prois
Vous en sucherez la goute
Vous qui ne goustez de pois

1

You must learn to eat cabbage
you who only eat peas

You must learn to eat cabbage
for the stepmother of three kings
can't engulf you with her ass
She must take the other route
because of an anal drip
that has captured her brown hole
she can't use a spike of green wheat
or anything else one might shove up there
to keep one's backside unsoiled
You'll discover a taste for it
you who only eat peas

Doucement me reconforte
Celle qui mon cuer a pris

Doucement me reconforte
Une chate a moitié morte
Qui chante touz les jeudis
Une alleluye si forte
Que li clichés de no porte
Dist que siens est li lendis
S'en fu uns leus si hardis
Qu'il ala maugré sa sorte
Tuer Dieu en Paradis
Et dist Compains je t'aporte
Celle qui mon cuer a pris

2

Gently she comforts me
the one who stole my heart

Gently she comforts me
a half-dead tabby cat
who sings every Thursday
a hallelujah so shrill
that the latch of our gate
says the tariff is his
& made a wolf so brave
he ran off despite his rank
to murder God in heaven
then said Friend I bring you
the one who stole my heart

Je me veul d'amour retraire
Puis qu'elle m'i fait languir

Je me veul d'amour retraire
Dist uns estrons mors a traire
Et dire voir pour mentir
Et si vestirai la haire
Desormais & pour pis faire
Me veul en bien convertir
Et quant j'orrai retentir
Le mortier & les aus faire
G'irai mes boiaus sentir
Car tel note me doit plaire
Puis qu'ele m'i fait languir

3

I want to flee from love
since it makes me feel so ill

I want to flee from love
said a dead turd still unshat
& speak the truth with lies
& if from now on I wear
the hair-shirt to worsen myself
I'll become a holy soul
& once I have heard the mortar
resound & crushed the garlic
I'll go smell my own bowels
for such an air must please me
since it makes me feel so ill

A *bonne amour sui donnee*
Mon vivant pour miex valoir

A *bonne amour sui donnee*
Quant une chievre damnee
M'a dit que je doi avoir
A fame une cheminee
Qui ne hume que pevree
Pour .i. ours s'i concevoir
C'on ne s'en puist percevoir
Mais s'elle est despucelee
Et je le puisse savoir
J'amerai une popee
Mon vivant pour miex valoir

4

I gave myself to true love
to make my life more worthy

I gave myself to true love
when a hell-bound nanny-goat
said that if I want a wife
I must marry a fireplace
who drinks only hot pepper
so a bear might conceive
what we cannot perceive
But if she's been deloused
& somehow I find out
I'll love a puppet instead
to make my life more worthy

Sans confort ne vivrai mie
De la douche longuement

Sans confort ne vivrai mie
Se vous ne baisiez demie
Sire de mon fondement
Et se li trous en lermie
Vous mascherez croste & mie
De ce breneus oingnement
D'entour si sarez comment
On destrempe tel boillie
Puis humés tout chaudement
Si porrez avoir copie
De la douce longuement

5

Comfortless I cannot live
on this simple fare for long

Comfortless I cannot live
if you kiss but one half
Sire of my fundament
& if the hole dribbles
you can smear this brown salve
eat it up with crusts & crumbs
If you know how to brew
such a hot & tasty broth
drink it quick straight from the pot
you won't get such jouissance
from this simple fare for long

Amis puis que vous partés
Toute ma joie est faillie

Amis puis que vous partés
J'arai .ii. eus esquatés
Qui devendront formaigie
Pour chanter a .ii. autés
Tant que vous serez autés
C'uns estrons mors qui rougie
Car une truie soingie
Dist hier a .iiii. pastés
Seigneur j'ai .i. cul qui chie
Mais s'a vo nés n'i tastés
Toute ma joie est faillie

6

Beloved since you left me
all my joy has been cast down

Beloved since you left me
I'll break a couple of eggs
to make a plate of cheeses
sing two notes in unison
& you will be raised as high
as a dead-bitten blushing turd
because a scrupulous sow
said yesterday to four cakes
My Lord I've an ass that shits
but since you've never savored it
all my joy has been cast down

Puis qu'il m'estuet de ma dame partir
Or voi je bien je pert soulas & joie

Puis qu'il m'estuet de ma dame partir
J'espouserai saint Pierre le martir
Pour engendrer .i. mahommé de croie
Qui me fera le tonnoirre engloutir
Et puis m'irai en Paradis quatir
Deci a tant que d'amer m'i recroie
Mais se g'i truis angle qui en Dieu croie
Je m'i voudrai de chanter aätir
Si haut que touz diront que je songoie
Quant le douz mal de mort ne puis sentir
Or voi je bien je pert soulas et joie

7

Because I have to leave my love
I must lose all comfort & joy
            – Guillaume de Machaut

Because I have to leave my love
I'll marry Saint Peter the martyr
& give birth to a plaster idol
who'll make me ingurgitate thunder
& then I'll go hide in Paradise
until love crucifies me again
If just one angel believed in God
I'd learn to sing a battle hymn
so loudly they'll all say I'm dreaming
When I cannot feel sweet pangs of death
I must lose all comfort & joy

Hé gracieuse au cors gent
Quant arés de moi merci

Hé gracieuse au cors gent
Uns leus a queue d'argent
A si le ventre entoumi
Qu'il n'a c'un oil & .i. dent
Et quant il vient entre gent
Tantost a Dieu endormi
& fait pour l'amour de mi
.I. si fort molin a vent
Desouz le pié d'un fourmi
Que li clichets dist Hersent
Quant arés de moi merci

8

Hey my voluptuous beauty
will you ever take pity on me

Hey my voluptuous beauty
a wolf with a silver tail
engorged his fat belly so much
he lost but one eye & one tooth
& when He walks among us
God falls asleep right away
& creates as my true love
such a powerful windmill
under the foot of an ant
that the latch says to the she-wolf
Will you ever take pity on me

Quant biautez dame a vous m'amaine
J'ai joie ramenee ici

Quant biautez dame a vous m'amaine
Dist la gueule d'un saint a laine
J'espouserai ochi ochi
Pour miex mengier fain & avaine
Et puis s'irai saignier a vaine
L'ombre de la tour de Couchi
Mais se li vins de Clamechi
Ne m'aprent la triquedondaine
Je frai au conte de Rouchi
Chanter ou cul d'une seraine
J'ai joie ramenee chi

9

My love when beauty brings you nigh
It brings my joy back to me

My love when beauty brings you nigh
said the maw of a hairy saint
I'll marry Ochi ochi
to eat better oats & hay
& then I'll cut open the veins
of the shadow of Couci tower
But if the wines of Clamecy
won't teach me to *triquedondaine*
I'll make the count of Rochy
sing in a mermaid's asshole
It brings my joy back to me

Douz viaire mon cuer avez
A touzjours mais parfaitement

Douz viaire mon cuer avez
Pour ce que vous ne vous lavez
Nulle fois sans .i. oingnement
De quoi je sui touz debavez
Mais se les rues n'en pavez
D'aval Paris certainement
Pais prendrez a mon fondement
Se le bren baisier n'en savez
Vous li dirés d'amendement
Par vostre oudeur conquis m'avez
A touzours mais parfaitement

10

Your sweet look captured my heart
forever & perfectly

Your sweet look captured my heart
for you never wash yourself
without this sticky ointment
I've drooled all over myself
But if the streets of Paris
are not paved with it surely
you'll give my ass the kiss of peace
If you won't taste its brown kiss
you must say to make amends
Your odor has conquered me
forever & perfectly

Ami loial vous ai trouvé
S'est drois qu'a vous me rende prise

Ami loial vous ai trouvé
Dame car .i. bués m'a couvé
Tant que je sui li vens de bise
C'on a pris pour larron prouvé
Pour ce que j'ai voie escouvé
Luxure hors de Sainte Eglyse
Que nus n'aimme au monde ne prise
S'en a si son cors esprouvé
Que toute en a arsse & esprise
La mer qui mon cuer m'a rouvé
S'est drois qu'a vous me rende prise

11

Faithful friend I have found you
& must place myself in your keep
                              – Jehan de le Mote

Faithful friend I have found you
because an ox hatched me my dear
I still chase after the north wind
who we all took for a known thief
because I swept luxury
out the doors of the Holy Church
which no one in this world could love
if his body were not so wracked
it burnt to tinder & ash
the bitter sea that begged my heart
to place itself in your keep

Amis se vous ne voulez boire
Je vous prie que vous humés

Amis se vous ne voulez boire
Dist la paireure d'une istoire
Il couvient que vous devinés
Se ma dame a talent de poire
Et puis remascherés la poire
Dont je fui hersoir desjunés
Tant c'uns mors chiens & traïnés
Fera en lui saint Jehan croire
Et dira Se vous ne junés
Sire vesci mon cul qui foire
Je vous prie que vous humés

12

Friend if you need a drink
please slake your thirst right here

Friend if you need a drink
said the sire of an anecdote
the moment has come to divine
if my Lady wants to fog the air
& thus remasticate the pear
I ate for breakfast late last night
so that a dog's tortured carcass
would make Saint John revere him
& say Sir if you're not fasting
here is my ass on holiday
please slake your thirst right here

Ma joie en douleur se mue quant
Pour humblement prier merci ne puis recouvrer

Ma joie en douleur se mue
Ce dist une vesse mue
Quant ne me puis delivrer
De chevauchier a sambue
Pour ce c'uns estrons qui bue
A fait vo gorge enyvrer
Mais g'irai tant abuvrer
Une vielz pelle cornue
Qu'elle ira dimenche ouvrer
Et crier aval no rue
Merci ne puis recouvrer

13

My joy is silenced by pain
when my humble prayers bring me no release

My joy is silenced by pain
so said an undischarged fart
for I can't relieve myself
while I'm riding side-saddle
because a turd doing laundry
inebriated your gorge
I'll get a thorny old pearl
so woefully plastered
she'll go to work on Sunday
& cry in the street below
Prayers bring me no release

Maugré felons mesdisans
Maintendrai le bien amer

Malgré felons mesdisans
Serai je si voirdisans
Que je m'en ferai blasmer
A .ii. fours demi cuisans
Qui devindrent clerc lisans
Pour une truie affamer
Et puis noierent en mer
Le songe des .VII. Dormans
Pour ce que ne volt chanter
Avec les petis enfans
Maintendrai le bien amer

14

In spite of gossiping thieves
I'll stand by the one I love

In spite of gossiping thieves
I'll be so honestly true
that I'll find myself condemned
by two half-baking ovens
who'd become bible reciters
to starve a scrawny porker
& then drown in the ocean
the Dream of the Seven Sleepers
Because he refused to sing
with all the little children
I'll stand by the one I love

En chantant me reconforte
Quant j'ai perdu mon ami

En chantant me reconforte
Une oë qui fu si forte
Qu'elle abati saint Remi
En luitant jambe torte
Mais uns limaçons l'emporte
As chans de Befabemi
Et puis dist A Elami
Va chacier dehors no porte
Le songe Pierre Remi
Et li di qu'envie est morte
Quant j'ai perdu mon ami

15

I find my solace in song
since I lost my one true friend
                              – Jehan de le Mote

I find solace in the song
of a goose who honked so loud
she razed Saint-Remi abbey
fighting with a sprained ankle
But a snail bore her away
atop a Doremifaso
& said Ah oh Mercy me
go & chase from our gates
the finance minister's dream
& tell him desire died
when I lost my one true friend

Plaisant regart de ma dame
Me fait amer de cuer vrai

Plaisant regart de ma dame
M'a fait de Remi tel game
Que la perte i recouvrai
D'un Escot a pié d'eschame
Qui mist a feu & a flame
Le temps qu'avec lui ouvrai
Mais ce c'ou bec li lairai
Les braies au cors saint Jame
Et que saint Pierre enjurai
Ainz qu'il eüst cors në ame
Me fait amer de cuer vrai

16

The sweet gaze of my beloved
makes me love with a true heart

The sweet gaze of my beloved
sent such a tune from Saint Remi
that our debt was recovered
from a peg-legged Scotsman
who put to fire & to flame
the gray weather he brought with him
because he'd left in his mouth
the pants from Saint James' corpse
& cursed out Saint Peter
before he had body or soul
it makes me love with a true heart

Ma dame que j'aim d'amour fine
Car me regardez de cuer fin

Ma dame que j'aim d'amour fine
Dist uns singes a la daufine
J'ai une teste d'esclefin
Qui m'a dit que Paradis fine
Et que li firmamens s'acline
A faire pape du dauffin
Mais se la taie d'un auffin
Pour mon escot ne paie & fine
Je li dirai se j'ai pris fin
Orde vielle puans rufine
Car me regardez de cuer fin

17

I love my Lady so truly
for she loves me with a pure heart

I love my Lady so truly
said an ape to the Dauphine
I have the head of a haddock
who told me Paradise ends
& that heaven feels inclined
to name as Pope our Dauphin
If a chess piece's grandmother
won't pay me my asking price
I'll tell her if I should die
You're a rank be-shitted bawd
for you love me with a pure heart

S'ensi est que ne vous voie
Ma tres douce dame gente

S'ensi est que ne vous voie
Ce dist uns singes qui noie
A une fueille de mente
Je serai cuens de Savoie
Car une vache de Troie
M'a donné le dons de rente
En l'ombre d'une piésente
Mais se c'est fausse monnoie
G'irai dire a une lente
Ostés vo cul qu'il ne poie
Ma tres douce dame gente

18

In case I don't see you again
my dear sweet gentle madam
                    – Guillaume de Machaut

In case I don't see you again
so said a drowning monkey
to a passing mint leaf
I'll be the count of Savoy
because a Trojan heifer
gave me love's sinecure
in the shade of a footpath
But if that is false coin
I'll tell a slow-witted louse
Haul ass whatever the weight
my dear sweet gentle madam

Je sui souvent pour ma dame en esmai
Quant je ne puis en li merci trouver

Je sui souvent pour ma dame en esmai
Quant uns oisons d'avril couvé en mai
Me fist hersoir en Paradis voler
Pour engendrer le cors saint Nicholai
....
Qui ne volt onques a Dieu merci rouver
Mais uns escouffles li dist sanz mot sonner
Biaus douz compains onques fort vin n'amai
Je te ferai d'un estront desjuner
Que je chiai ens ou bois de Mormai
Quant je ne puis en li merci trouver

19

My love often has me in dismay
when I can find no mercy in her

My love often has me in dismay
since an April gosling hatched in May
last night flew me up to Paradise
to give birth to Saint Nicholas's corpse
....
who'd never stoop to beg God's mercy
but a hawk said to him without a word
My dear friend I never liked strong wine
For breakfast I will feed you a turd
that I shat in the woods of Mormai
when I could find no mercy in her

A fine amour devendrai fins amis
Pour estre miex amez d'amie fine

A fine amour devendrai fins amis
Car une truie vestue de samis
Me fist hersoir engendrer me marrine
Qui m'a apris a buier les tamis
Et uns hairons qui est en fierte mis
Devint tantost mestre de medecine
Tu as menti dist uns harens d'espine
. . . .
Et je m'en vois preschier en la Champine
Et confesser les pourciaus endormis
Pour estre miex amez d'amie fine

20

Of perfect love make perfect friendship
to be better loved by a perfect friend

Of perfect love make perfect friendship
for a battering ram in Syrian silks
last night made me father my godmother
who taught me the art of puncturing sieves
& a heron sealed up in a tomb
became a doctor of medicine
A hawthorn herring said You lied
. . . .
& I'll go preach about it in Champagne
& take confession from sleeping piglets
to be better loved by a perfect friend

Ma dame vostre veüe
M'a de vous amer espris

Ma dame vostre veüe
Ce dist une besagüe
Trouva hier en ses escris
C'une singesse cornue
Est abesse devenue
De Saint Antoine a Paris
Mais Diex en geta .i. ris
Car toute joie ot perdue
Pour ce c'uns eus de pertris
Me dist c'uns estrons de grue
M'a de bien amer espris

21

The brightness of your look
set me on fire with love
                    – Lescutel

The brightness of your look
so said a two-sided axe
who lately found in his book
that a monkey with horns
became Mother Superior
of Saint Anthony's hospice
God got a laugh out of it
because all His joy was lost
when the egg of a cock partridge
said that the dung of a crane
had set me afire with love

La grant biauté dame de vostre face
M'esprent de vous servir & bien amer

La grant biauté dame de vostre face
A pris .i. chat qui .iiii. leus enchace
Et si m'a fait un tel brouet humer
Que g'engendrai Guillaume Fierebrace
Qui m'envoia chanter de geste en place
Tant que j'apris les porciaus a tumber
Mais quant je vi la taie saint Omer
Qui chevauchoit le picot d'une eschace
Je l'envoiai en enfer sarmonner
Pour convertir .i. fol qui de sa mace
Merci me fait doucement esperer

22

Lady the great beauty of your face
inflamed me to love & serve you well

Lady the great beauty of your face
caught a cat being chased by four wolves
& forced me to drink such a broth
that I gave birth to Guillaume Fierebrace
who exiled me to sing epics at home
provided I teach pigs acrobatics
When I beheld Saint Omer's grandmother
riding high on the head of a crutch
I sent her down to give sermons in hell
to convert a dimwit whose war-hammer
gave me some hope for tender mercy

Dame de grant biauté parfaite
Je vous aime parfaitement

Dame de grant biauté parfaite
Dist une truie contrefaite
Vous baiserez mon fondement
S'ensi est qu nus vous ▮▮▮▮
Car une vielz maison desfaite
M'en a raporté jugement
Pour ce c'uns ombres de jument
De combatre a .i. koc s'afaite
Pour armer dist seürement
Une vesse en vo gorge faite
Je vous aime parfaitement

23

Lady of perfect beauty
I love you perfectly

Lady of perfect beauty
said a counterfeit sow
you'll kiss my fundament
which is how no one ███ you
for an old house in ruins
pronounced sentence on me
because the shade of a mare
preparing to fight a cock
said firmly to steel her soul
Fart just once with your throat
& I'll love you perfectly

Amis ne te desconforte
Mais aies ton cuer en joie

Amis ne te desconforte
J'arai une chievre morte
Pour .i. sor harenc qui noie
Qui veillera a ta porte
C'uns limachons ne t'enporte
Et s'ensi est que je poie
Tu diras .i. chien de croie
S'il te mort qu'il me deporte
Et s'aucuns pendre t'envoie
N'en pleure ja lerme forte
Mais aies ton cuer en joie

24

Do not despair my friend
but be of joyful heart

Do not despair my friend
I'll get a dead nanny-goat
traded for a drowned kipper
to keep watch at your door
so no snail will kidnap you
If by chance I should fart
you'll tell a dog of the cross
to forgive me if he bites you
& if someone sends you to hang
cry your acrid tears no more
but be of joyful heart

J'aim par amors c'onques Dieu ne sa mere
Ne touz si saint n'i puissent avoir part

J'aim par amors c'onques Diex ne sa mere
Ne porent faire une oë si amere
Que je n'i aie engendré .i. poupart
Qui me menra la queue d'une aree
Car j'apris hier l'afaire & le mistere
De boire toute l'yaue qui se depart
Mais quant je vi le songe d'un liepart
Qui ███ ██ le fuisiau sa commere
Je dis Compains mes cuers de vous se part
Se vous ne faites si que brués vo père
Ne touz si sains n'i puissent avoir part

25

I love by love without God or his mother
or any of the saints who played a part

I love by love without God or his mother
enough to get a goose so heated up
that she made me give birth to a puppet
who then brought me the shaft of a plough
for yesterday I learned the secret art
of drinking all the drainage waters
But when I see the dream of a leopard
who ▆▆ ▆▆ his grandmother's spindle
I say Friend my heart takes leave of you
if you do nothing but burn your father
or any of the saints who played a part

Presidentes in tronis seculi
Sunt hodie dolus & rapina

Presidentes in tronis seculi
Ce dist uns eus armez de cuir boilli
En cop de ▇▇ si grant medecine a
C'une charrete jusqu'a Mes en sailli
Qui engendra le seigneur de Seulli
La Maselaine dont uns cos se disna
Mais uns harens touz s'en desgratina
Quant il fu mors pour ce c'on li toli
La pater nostre qui li adevina
Qu'avec les angles *in gloria celi*
Sunt hodie dolus et rapina

26

Presidentes in tronis seculi
Sunt hodie dolus & rapina †

Presidentes in tronis seculi
so said an eyeball armored in leather
one cup of ▇ was such good medicine
a cart who begot the Lord of Souilly
jumped from here all the way out to Metz
& dined with a dupe on St Madelaine's day
But a kipper scraped off his own scales
after his death because someone revoked
the paternoster which promised him that
with the angels *in gloria celi*
sunt hodie dolus & rapina

† *Masters who reign over the world*
today deceit & plunder prevail

Tant est amours vertus noble et poissans
Qu'elle a sour touz seignorie et poissance

Tant est amours vertus noble et poissans
Dist uns sirons plus gros que li croissans
Qu'elle me fait couler parmi la pance
La haute mer et les poissons noans
Et s'afaitast une paire de gans
Prince de Gale & roÿne de France
Mais g'en ferai Dieu peser en balance
S'il ne me fait a lui estre semblans
Plaindre m'irai a .i. coutiau sanz mance
Pour ce c'une oe est si outrecuidans
Qu'elle a seur touz seignorie & poissance

27

Love is so virtuous noble & strong
she has rule & power over all things

Love is so virtuous noble & strong
said a flea bigger than the crescent moon
She made the high sea & swimming fishes
spill out all over my potbelly
& would anoint a pair of mittens
Prince of Wales & Queen of France
But I'll make God weigh them in the balance
if He won't fashion me in His image
I'll complain to a knife with no handle
because a barnyard goose got so haughty
she has rule & power over all things

Ma dame se j'ai pestri
Vous arés de mon bis pain

Ma dame se j'ai pestris
J'arai deus oés de pertris
Qui seront fil de nonnain
Et s'aront piet de brebis
Pour ce que .ii. moines bis
Furent hersoir pris a l'ain
Maugré le cors saint Gilain
Qui pria a .ii. rubis
Venés moi tendre la main
As Innocens a Paris
Vous arés de mon bis pain

28

My Lady if I've kneaded well
you'll have some of my brown bread

My Lady if I've kneaded well
I will have two partridge eggs
who'll be the sons of a nun
with the cloven hoofs of sheep
because two Franciscan monks
last night were caught on a hook
despite the corpse of Saint Giles
who'd prayed on his two rubies
Come here & give me your hand
at Les Innocents in Paris
you'll have some of my brown bread

Amis amés de cuer d'amie
Amez comme loiaus amis

Amis amez de cuer d'amie
Je vous lirai d'astronomie
Ce dist .i. ours a .ii. tamis
Qui avoient l'ost estourmie
Et s'aprendrai tant d'escremie
Que la despoille d'un fourmis
Desconfira nos anemis
Et se je voi oe & demie
Je li dirai Cuers endormis
L'ombre d'une truie endormie
Amés com fins loiaus amis

29

Lover loved with a lover's heart
love like a faithful lover

Lover loved with a lover's heart
I will teach you astronomy
so said a bear to two sieves
who had called an army to arms
& you will learn such swordplay
that the clothes of an ant stripped bare
will disconcert our enemies
& if I see a goose & a half
I will tell her Dear heart asleep
in the shade of a catapult
love like a faithful lover

Amours pour quoi m'avez prise
Et que vous ai ge mesfait

Amours pour quoi m'avez prise
Ce dist une oë de Frise
Je n'ai vaillant c'un souhait
& s'alai hier a l'eglyse
Toute nue sans chemise
Espouser .i. vel de lait
Pour ce c'uns oignons qui brait
Se combatoit a la bise
Et li dist Sire entresait
S'uns estrons les dens vous brise
Et que vous ai ge mesfait

30

Love why have you seized me
& how have I done you wrong

Love why have you seized me
so said a Frisian goose
I have just one wish that counts
& yesterday I went to church
shirtless & completely bare
to marry a dairy cow
because a screaming onion
battled the north-eastern wind
& said Sire I am sure
you cracked your teeth on a turd
& how have I done you wrong

Explicit les Fastras

Afterword

by Donato Mancini

Je versefie en dormant / I write poems in my sleep

Long-forgotten, ill-respected, short lived. Until recently, these words could have characterized the reception history of the *fatrasies* and *fatras*, a small corpus of intricate "nonsense" poems written between 1250 and 1330 in Northern France. The 54th stanza of the set known as the *Fatrasies d'Arras* (*Fatrasies of Arras*) — the "famous stanza," as Patrice Uhl describes it[1] — is cited in many critical texts and anthologies, and is often presented with little or no commentary.

Uns ours emplumés	A feathered bear
Fist semer uns blés	sowed a field of wheat
De Douvre a Wissent	from Dover to Calais
Uns oingnons pelez	A peeled onion
Estoit aprestés	was getting warmed up
De chanter devant	to lead with a song
Qant sor .i. rouge olifant	when atop a red elephant
Vint uns limeçons armés	came a heavily-armed snail
Qui lor aloit escriant	who ran around shouting
Fil a putain sa venez	Son of a bitch Bring it on
Je versefie en dormant	I write poems in my sleep

In this un-anecdote, impossible activities set the stage for impossible actions which, just as they're about to be realized, are averted by miraculous intervention[2]. In spite of the first impression of confusion, nothing here is actually incoherent.[3] But, rather than being unified by topic or through narrative continuity, the stanza knits together with several overlapping motifs: time, movement, vocal sounds, and food. Broader coherence is drawn by arranging the protagonists into two distinct categories: (1) Large, strong animal with an extraordinary characteristic (feathered bear; red elephant); and (2) Small, ordinary food item with the ability to make loud vocal sounds (singing onion; shouting escargot). Scale is warped out of proportion, in the way that it often is in dreams. A lone bear sows wheat across 30 miles, a difficult job even if the distance didn't span the English Channel. The smallest animal, the snail, commands the largest, the elephant. Spatial relationships are undecidably ambiguous. The peeled onion is warmed up and ready to sing *devant* (out front), but out front of what? Where are any of the protagonists even situated, in relation to each other? The actions in the latter 8 lines the poem are transitory, hypothetical or unrealized. It seems like the latter parts of the poem, in fact, set up an activity that will begin after its conclusion: a poetry battle between agri-aqua-bird-bear, canto-onion and war-snail. Although the poem isn't specific enough to be political satire, these unreal acts and relationships are staged within the political realities of intra-European conflict (specifically, the long series of Franco-English wars, triggered again in 1294) and European religious imperialism (specifically, the Crusades, the ninth of which starts in 1271). Note that the elephant, standing in to some extent for "the East," would be exotic in a fatrasie even if the elephant weren't red. Most of the protagonists and objects of this corpus are from French medieval everyday life: from barnyards or kitchens, from local forests or local churches, from bedroom or town square.

Semantically coherent and referentially dense, yet without making discursive or narrative "sense," the fatrasies and fatras are also consistent across the corpus. Many individual stanzas from the core set could be used to introduce them all. *Fatrasies d'Arras* 54 (FA 54) was singled out early on, however, for at least one good reason: it punctuates. Concluding the *Fatrasies d'Arras*, it is also the last surviving fatrasie stanza, before the archive shows the fatrasie developing to become a different form, the fatras.[4] In a fatras, a fatrasie-like 11-line poem is built by sandwiching nine newly written lines between the first and second lines of a pre-written couplet. The couplet and the filler lines are in contrasting registers: the new lines are mutant, chimerical; the framing couplet is courtly, proverbial, even clichéd. This dialogic interplay of registers gives credence to the critical view that the fatrasies and the fatras were written collaboratively, following strict rules that diffract individual creative control.

Part of the comic appeal of the final line of FA 54 is that the warlike snail is bragging, within the strictures of a fixed verse-form, that he finds poetry laughably easy to write. Coming as it does at the end of the series, the line also does much more. As Bettina Full suggests, it seems reasonable to read this concluding stanza as a reflection on the whole fatrastic corpus. In this stanza, particularly its final line, the fatrasie emerges, retrospectively, as both an account of dream visions and as the product of a rigorous compositional procedure.[5] Linking the fatrasies and fatras with the medieval tradition of writing about, and through, dreams, FA 54 also thus puts the poems into a doubled historical perspective, touching both their antiquity and their startling modernity.[6]

In French poetry of the thirteenth and fourteenth centuries, the dream was a prominent device. Dreams were, in the words of medievalist Michel Zink, "the means ... nearly always used to place the [poetic] subject into the allegorical world".[7] A signal example is found in the first section of the *Roman de la Rose* (c. 1230), which opens with the poet retelling a transformative dream from years past, before proceeding to interpret that dream from the perspective of his wiser, present self.[8] With the line "Je versefie en dormant," the anonymous writers of the *Fatrasies d'Arras* — perhaps as a joke, but perhaps as an actual statement of method, or even as both — evoke a technique called *dorveille* or "sleepwake." As Zink writes, *dorveille* was developed for long journeys on horseback, allowing a mounted rider to ride on past exhaustion. It is "a sort of drowsiness," Zink explains, "in which the mind maintains only a distant relationship with reality or even loses contact with it, but without actually giving way to sleep."[9] *Dorveille* was adopted as a trope in dream-poetry, and was literally adopted by some as a "creative means" for writing poetry.[10] In the fatrasies and fatras, dreams and sleep are mentioned numerous times, often in the frame of wakeful sleep. The shadow of a washtub sleeps to stay more awake. A donkey's dreams bray out a fire alert. Significantly, there is another mention of composing poetry through dream:

Dui rat userier	Two usurious rats
Voloient songier	hoped that in dreaming
Por faire .i. descort	they'd write a descort[11]

The methodical, rule-bound generation of poetic chimeras is arguably unique in medieval poetry to the fatrasies and fatras, raising questions about the poems' meaning and intent.

In the thirteenth century, practices of literary dream-analysis were predominantly based in the writings of the fifth-century thinker Macrobius. In his commentary on Cicero's *Somnium Scipionis* (Dream of Scipio), Macrobius names five kinds of dream, only three of which he considers legitimate for allegorical interpretation.[12] Within the Macrobian tradition, one could say that the fatrasies and fatras dream, but that they dream illicitly. Although composed using some kind of systematic method — the precise mechanics of which can only be guessed at — fatrasies appear, to cite Zink again, like "*phantasmata* [Latin: *visum/visa*]... the disjointed or indistinct images that present themselves in the intermediate state between waking and slumber, at the moment of falling asleep."[13] In Macrobius's system, unlike the enigmatic *enupnion* [Latin: *insomnium*], which conceal meaning with "strange shapes," *phantasmata* "allow no interpretation and conceal no truth."[14] As Lambert C. Porter writes, after it disappears in the fourteenth century, such a poetics of *phantasmata* would rarely be seen again until the emergence of Modernism in the twentieth.[15]

Scholars have compared the fatrasies and fatras with the works of a range of twentieth century artistic movements, including Cubism (c. 1907), Dada (1917), and Oulipo (1960). The comparison made most often, by far, is with Dada's first child, Surrealism (c. 1920).[16] Surrealism is prominent here partly because the Surrealists developed a comprehensive poetics and methodology of the dream. Like the fatrasies, many Surrealist texts never actually leave the space of dream. Both dwell, by mandate, in a world of the impossible, where dream is means and end, without exit. With its droll but true declaration of method, *FA 54* brings the fatrasiers close — for many, uncomfortably so — to André Breton and company. Recall the anecdote Breton tells in his *Manifeste du surréalisme* (1924), about the poet Saint-Pol-Roux. Saint-Pol-Roux was known to hang a sign on this bedroom door while he slept: "POET AT WORK."[17] "Je versefie en dormant" sets the fatrasies and fatras into the context of medieval practice — albeit at the outer limits of that very context — while pointing ahead to their "poetically troubling" (Pierre Bec), likeness with Modernism. As Uhl emphasizes, this likeness has proven awkwardly unmanageable for medievalists, just as the fatrasies must have been unmanageable for the literati of the thirteenth century.[18]

The strangeness of these poems has even compelled some, such as the medievalist and historian Jean Dufournet, to identify in the fatrasies and fatras a pseudo-Modernist "poetics of rupture," one that "empties" words of their instrumental meanings in order to "give birth" to a new language.[19] From Dufournet's perspective, the emergence of the *fatrasique* (fatrastic) marks the beginning-of-the-end of an ancient literary tradition, an early threshold of the modern in French literature. For Paul Zumthor, one of the first widely influential scholars to work on these poems, they were even more: the actual beginning of modern poetry in Europe, a true *ars nova*.[20]

With such an attractively controversial profile, why are the fatrasies and fatras not already a well-known part of the history of innovative literatures? Why were they set aside for so long, virtually delaying their reception until the twentieth century? And what does it mean to read them today, over a century after the word *sur-réalisme* first appeared in print?

Un sens sans mimoyre / A mind without memory

The only substantial clues readers today have about the initial writing, transmission and reception of the fatrasies and fatras are in their source manuscripts, the biographies of their authors, and in the intertextual afterlives of the two forms. For a very long time, the last public notice of the fatras was given by poet Louis Du Gardin, in his handbook of French versification *Les Premières addresses du chemin de Parnasse* (1620). Du Gardin presents a single, mediocre fatras as an example of a long-dead poetic form, little more than "an old poem."[21] In consigning the fatras to the forgettable past, Du Gardin followed a path laid by other poeticians in the fifteenth century. Jean Molinet — ironically, one of the last prolific writers of fatras, credited by some as the form's "liquidator" (Uhl) — in his *Art de rhétorique* (1492) had already dismissed the fatras as "not recommended … avoided by good artists."[22] The peak period for the fatrasie and fatras extends only from the 1250s, in Arras (fatrasies), to the 1330s, in Paris (fatras); as Uhl observes, interest in the truly fatrastic must have already begun to cool as early as the 1330s.[23] Not even the poets who continued writing fatras into the fifteenth century seem to have been aware of the fatrasie, as attested by the complete absence of this word from their otherwise comprehensive poetics manuals.[24] Furthermore, nearly all the fatras that survive from after 1330 are what critics have called, following Baudet Harenc's *Le doctrinal de la seconde rhétorique* (1432), "possible" (reasonable, sensible, rational, versus "impossible") fatras. These later fatras, written by poets like Harenc, Molinet and Du Gardin, are pedagogical exercises, or imaginatively listless imitations of the form used ornamentally in playscripts.[25]

To medievalist Giovanna Angeli, the afterlife of the fatrasie is a story of its recuperation. It is a taming, a trivialization or an emptying-out of the fatrastic, as the fatrasie develops to become the fatras.[26] Angeli considers the fatrasies some of the most radical texts of the French Middle Ages. So, too, do many others, including Martijn Rus, a recent editor-translator of the fatrasies. Rus maintains that these poets went further along the path of poetic exploration than any other writers of their time.[27] For Angeli, in the development from fatrasie to fatras, the fatrastic is re-absorbed into the poetic culture that it had strived to escape. Certainly, the fatras is a hybrid form, with elements of phantasmagoric ambiguity and of burlesque parody.[28] In the fatras, "nonsense and buffoonery alternate" quickly, unpredictably, unsystematically.[29] For Angeli, this development is a regression. As if to contain the excesses of these "texts without images" (Pierre Jourde), the delirious, extravagant, mendacious fatrasie is given a satirical frame, a "head and a tail."[30]

And yet for some writers, it still seemed possible, well over a century after its appearance, to use the fatras to emblematize deranged or demonic speech. As if in memory of irrational, blasphemous, "impossible" fatras, Guillaume Flamang, in his *Vie et passion de Monseigneur Sainct Didier* (1482), writes a "possible" but chthonic fatras into the mouths of Satan and Lucifer themselves. The two devils bawl together:

Raillez criez horriblement	Jeer and cry out horribly
O faulce caterve infernalle	O false infernal congregation[31]

Even if the fatrastic was domesticated, the poems, or their memory, remained frightful and unwelcome to some. A caged demon is still a demon.

For modern readers, the slow process of these poems' revival is begun by Achille Jubinal, who includes the *Fatrasies d'Arras* in an anthology first published in 1839.[32] The return of the fatrastic was not initially celebrated by medievalists. In 1868, Auguste Scheler set the tone for their reception, calling the fatras "insipid" non-sequiturs that did not even reach the level of "mental debauchery."[33] Decades later, in an entry for the *Histoire littéraire de la France* (1921), Charles-Victor Langlois expresses a similarly exaggerated revulsion. Although obscenity was constant, even requisite, in French medieval comic literature, Langlois claims that "never, anywhere, has such repugnant scatology been so pervasive" as it is in the fatras.[34] In this ambiance, no sustained scholarly work would appear before 1938, when Leonard E. Arnaud submits a little-known, rarely cited English-language dissertation on the fatrasies and fatras at New York University. In his thesis, Arnaud situates fatrastic poetics in relation to other poetry of the period, anticipating later scholarship on many points. Unlike later scholars, however, Arnaud expresses naked contempt for most of the corpus. To Arnaud, simple games of absurd juxtaposition mixed with a "liberal quantity of smut" make up the "whole bag of tricks" of the fatrastic.[35]

Before Arnaud, Langlois's harsh judgement was exactly contemporaneous with a competing cultural tendency, already noted: the emergence of Dada and Surrealism. Through the Paris-based Surrealists, the fatrastic corpus found its first sympathetic public in many centuries, when issue no.6 of *La Révolution surréaliste* (March 1926) included some of these poems in translations by Georges Bataille.[36] Breton's reception of the poems, in private correspondence with Bataille, is a sign of the shift in values underway. Breton judges them "the most beautiful of all things."[37] Michel Leiris, who solicited the translations from Bataille, likewise (although much later) called the fatrasies "masterpieces of nonsense."[38] As Rus has noted, it was only with their endorsement by the Surrealists that some readers, including scholars, began to realize that contempt for these poems was undeserved and ill-motivated.[39] Yet the scholarly reception of the fatrasies and fatras only starts to broadly change tenor after 1960, when Porter publishes his comprehensive edition. Although the reception becomes much more generous after Porter, its problems are compounded by the "shadow of Bataille" (Uhl) that still accompanies the poems. To approach the fatrasies and fatras, scholars are forced to consider the intertwined, prickly questions of how to judge Surrealism, and how to deal with Surrealism's unlikely relationship with the fatrastic.

Chançons em poree / Songs in leek pottage

In a fatrasie, the goal is to construct a series of semantic contradictions and dream-like impossibilities, to tell lavishly unreal "anti-stories" by fusing as many semantic, logical and narrative incongruities as can fit into 65 syllables. Their un-anecdotes are told in correct meter and "impeccable grammar" (Uhl) that, to paraphrase Breton's words about Surrealist style, never deprives conventional syntax of its "rights."[40] The *strophe*, or stanza form, of the fatrasie is compactly dynamic: 6 lines of 5 syllables, in two groups of 3, followed by 5 lines of 7 syllables. With the rhyme scheme included, the form can be annotated:[41]

$$a^5 \ a^5 \ b^5 + a^5 \ a^5 \ b^5 \ // \ b^7 \ a^7 \ b^7 \ a^7 \ b^7$$

As Angeli noticed, the fatrasie's *strophe* appears to be the product of a collage.[42] It looks as if two stanzas in different meters have been spliced together.[43]

Since the late 1980s, Uhl has maintained that the term fatrasie refers not to the individual 11-line stanzas (as Jubinal and Porter assumed), but to groups of 11 fatrastic stanzas. If so, 1 fatrasie = 11 stanzas of 11 lines.[44] By Uhl's count, 6 fatrasies survive. In the older system for counting the poems, used in Porter's and in Rus's editions, there are 66. The first (or first eleven) is by the poet Philippe de Rémi (d. 1265)[45], a knight at the court of the Countess Mahaut, in Arras. 5 (or 55) more, the *Fatrasies d'Arras*, were written by an anonymous collective, probably between 1280 and 1300.[46] Rémi is believed to have invented the fatrasie.[47] Notably, he also invented another "irrational" poetry form, the *resverie* (reverie).[48] Among the pieces translated by Bataille, along with FA 54, was the first stanza of Rémi's fatrasie. Like FA 54, it offers an example of the stanza-form, rhetorical devices and lexicon that is signature of the fatrastic:

Li chan d'une raine	A tree frog's song
Saine une balaine	drew blood from a whale
Ou fons de la mer	on the ocean floor
& une seraine	while a water nymph

Si emportoit Saine	hoisted the Seine
Deseur Saint Omer	beyond Saint-Omer
Uns muiau i vint chanter	A mute arrived singing
Sans mot dire a haute alaine	wordlessly as loud as he could
Se ne fust Warnaviler	If not for Warnavillers
Noié fuissent en le vaine	they'd have drowned in the veins
D'une teste de sengler	of the head of a wild boar

Governed by a "rule of absolute surprise,"[49] with each line a fatrastic narrative becomes more and more disjunctive, irrational, irreal — "impossible," to again use Harenc's term. As Uhl has said, wryly alluding to Arthur Rimbaud's visionary mandate, a fatrasie is a formally immaculate *raisonné dérèglement* (reasoned derangement).[50]

More than any other texts of their time, the fatrasies opened a path out of what Dufournet calls the rigid and stereotyped idiom of courtly poetry.[51] Fatrasies lack metaphysics, and lack second-order spiritual meanings.[52] They use few philosophical abstractions or personifications. Fatrasies lack similes, and contain no extended metaphors. None of the fatrasies are about courtly poetry's main topic, love. Eschewing love, they also eschew one of the predominant signifying devices of the period, allegory. Although the fatrasies are outliers in a tradition of dream poetics, where love, dream, heroism and allegory were tightly linked, none of the scholars who have written about these poems interprets them as allegorical. The fatrasies swarm with agential body fragments, talking objects, talking animals and sentient substances, but these are presented as magically roving shards of everyday life, not as figurations or as personifications. For Zumthor, as well as for literary critic Pierre Jourde, fatrastic protagonists are in fact anti-figures who neutralize, or even destroy, metaphor and metonymy.[53]

One aspect of fatrastic comedy, of the game it played, was to elicit medieval readers' practice of explaining literary dreams allegorically. But the fatrasie hints at allegorical meaning only so that it can disappoint, or defeat, explication. It is not hard to recognize that this is a core aspect of what was radical in the fatrasies. The semiotic research collective *Groupe μ*, in fact, conclude in their *Rhétorique de la poésie* (1990), that the refined delirium of the fatrasie must have been experienced as quasi-Satanic: "To humanize inanimate objects, to thingify the human or to animalize things (and, what's more, to do this to body parts and to fragments of objects), is to paint a grotesque picture of Creation. In an intensely Christian social context, the fatrasie therefore takes on a diabolical cast."[54] To the extent that the fatrasies are even parodies, they distantly parody the hyperbolic, magical acts of saints and epic heroes.[55] In the fatrasies, the only war heroes are absurd ones. A pickled herring besieges a castle from all sides. A blade of straw undermines a castle bastion. Or the armed snail intervenes, like a god, to divert the course of an already absurd destiny. As Full notes, snails in poetry often symbolized cowardice and weakness.[56] In making the snail a miraculous savior of the ridiculous, these poems push back against allegorical reading practices, taunting a poetic culture that celebrated idealized love, prophetic dreams and mythical violence.[57] As Angeli writes, the fatrasies must have therefore appeared to some like "the result of a diabolical intrigue," to others as a powerful "liberatory act."[58]

Andoille de voirre aprestoit son oyrre / A sausage of glass was packing its bags

Sometime around 1318, a form develops that appears to be a hybrid of a form called the *sotte chanson* (crazy song) and the fatrasie.[59] This new form is the fatras, or, in technical terms introduced by later poeticians, the *fatras enté* (grafted fatras).[60] Grafted fatras share all those qualities of the fatrasies enumerated above, with one decisive difference: the banished topic of love returns, to be ridiculed. *Sotte chansons* are "crazy," often obscene, parodies of love lyrics. In the transformation from fatrasie to fatras, a fatrastic stanza is "grafted" onto a couplet written (often, but not exclusively) in the register of courtly love. The first known grafted fatras are found in the richly illuminated manuscript of the *Roman de Fauvel* (c. 1316), signed by Chaillou de Pesstain. The most important single cache of grafted fatras, by far, is the group of 30 "impossible" fatras collected with the works of the *ménestrel* Watriquet de Couvin.[61] Yolanda Plumley presents evidence from Watriquet's other writings that he knew the *Fauvel* codex first-hand, and it may be there that he learned how to graft a fatras.[62] But it is crucial to note that Watriquet's fatras were written in collaboration with someone named Raimmondin — presumably a *jongleur* (an itinerant poet–musician–performer) — who may have already been versed in the fatras.

As in a fatrasie, every line of a fatras leaps away from the previous line, in bizarre non-sequiturs, dream-like shifts of scale or person, scatological or blasphemous jokes. A fatras performs a hallucinatory, babbling slapstick. In lines of 7, 8, or 10 syllables, with the same rhyme scheme as the fatrasie, a grafted fatras unfolds as follows:

A B   A a b a a b b a b a B

In their written form, the refrain couplet is stated once (AB). The first line of the couplet is then repeated (A), after which 9 new lines are inserted, followed with a reiteration of the second borrowed line (B). Watriquet and Raimmondin's second fatras is one of the most often cited, exemplary of the form's antiquity, its modernity, and its heightened carnival atmosphere:

Doucement me reconforte	*Gently she comforts me*
Celle qui mon cuer a pris	*the one who stole my heart*
Doucement me reconforte	*Gently she comforts me*
Une chate a moitié morte	a half-dead tabby cat
Qui chante touz les jeudis	who sings every Thursday
Une alleluye si forte	a hallelujah so shrill
Que li clichés de no porte	that the latch of our gate
Dist que siens est li lendis	says the tariff is his
S'en fu uns leus si hardis	& made a wolf so brave
Qu'il ala maugré sa sorte	he ran off despite his rank
Tuer Dieu en Paradis	to murder God in heaven
Et dist Compains je t'aporte	then said Friend I bring you
Celle qui mon cuer a pris	*the one who stole my heart*

In its first known occurrence, in Watriquet's *Dits de la cygoigne* (Poem of the Swan), the word "fatras" refers to the literary form, where it is already associated with frivolity.[63] According to Plumley, the word aptly describes the compositional procedure: "the term *fastras* is thought to derive from the verb 'farcir' ('to stuff'), so that, in effect, each nonsense verse 'stuffs' "[64] the refrain — like stuffing a sausage-skin.[65] Full adds that the etymology of the related word, fatrasie, remains controversial. "Fatrasie" may derive not from "stuff" but from *fantasie* (fantasy), which is to say *phantasma*. What counts most, she reasons, is that both possible origins are relevant.[66] A *fatras enté* can be thought of as a mix of fatrastic *phantasmata* and of scatological parody, a perverse mix of weightless dreams and grotesquely fecundating, mutated, fetid bodies: a fantasy-sausage.

Uns biaus hom sans teste / A handsome headless man

Although next to nothing is known about the public life of the fatrasies, the (thin) evidence around Watriquet and

Raimmondin's fatras can afford some insight. Collaborative authorship is among the key principles that unite the fatrasies with the fatras, across their distinct contexts. Philippe de Rémi may have invented the fatrasie alone, but the "generative structure" (Zumthor) of the fatrasie, which permits an infinite number of combinations from a finite set of rules,[67] immediately lent itself to collaborative writing practices. The consensus today is that the *Fatrasies d'Arras* were written by a "coterie" (Zumthor), probably formed through the *puys* of Arras. A *puy* was a poetry society, through which municipal poetry competitions and performances were organized. Many towns in Northern France had puys, and the puys of Arras were especially well-established and active.[68] Poetry was, in fact, a sensation in Arras of the period. It was a city where "everybody rhymes."[69] As Michèle Gally writes, the predominant taste was for poetry that could be exercised as an energetic, competitive language game.[70] Other collaborative forms were cultivated alongside the fatrasie. Among the best-documented is the *jeu-parti*, a competitive debate-form that involved two poets trading stanzas.[71] As Uhl notes, the more parodic of the surviving *jeux-partis* verge on the fatrastic.[72] More pointedly, the other "irrational" form Rémi invented, the *resverie*, is believed to have been written by a process not-so-distantly analogous to the Surrealists' *cadavre exquis* (exquisite corpse).[73] In this hothouse environment, as Zumthor argues, even if Rémi had no collaborators in writing the first fatrasie, the form was soon assimilated for a playful collectivity.[74] Whatever the concrete truth about how they were written, and by whom, the *je* who wrote the *Fatrasies d'Arras* "while asleep" was a collective *je*: handsome, but all body, with no head.

When the fatrasie moves from the circles of the Arras puys to the royal court in Paris, it does so only in its later incarnation, as the grafted fatras. The Watriquet-Raimmondin fatras are found in only one of the seven manuscripts that contain Watriquet's collected works.[75] It is assumed that, in contrast to the coteries of Arras, the less intricate but more speed-freaky, lithe, magnificently ass-backward fatras probably entertained a different kind of public, less exacting and one "fond of festive laughter."[76] The Watriquet manuscript states that they were, in fact, performed at court: "Here begin the fastras that Raimmondin and Watriquet debated on Easter day before the king, Philippe [VI] of France."[77] In performance, the 9 new lines of the grafted fatras were probably declaimed, and may have been improvised on the spot, while the refrains were probably sung.[78] (In contrast, a fatrasie, written assiduously, as Uhl suggests, "in the silence of the studio"[79], may have been recited at a public gathering but was probably not sung.) To picture the burlesque performance context, consider that the king himself is the probable addressee, the "Sire" in Watriquet and Raimmondin's final fatras: "Sire I am sure / you cracked your teeth on a turd / & how have I done you wrong."

Very little is known about Watriquet or his life, except what can be deduced from his writings. Not even his birth date or death date is known. His collected poems include a number of important and linguistically playful dream-poems, like the *Dit de l'araignée et du crapaud* (Poem of the Spider and the Toad) and *Miroir des Dames* (Mirror of Ladies), but the fatras are his only "impossible" poems, and his only known collaborations. Absolutely nothing is known about Raimmondin, beyond his association with these poems. Raimmondin is only assumed to have been a jongleur because "Raimmondin" sounds like the kind of sobriquet these travelling poets gave themselves.[80] The debate form seen in the fatras, however, does seem typical of the kinds of dialogic, improvisatory performances demanded of jongleurs at the time.[81] Porter believes, in fact, that the fatras was probably invented by some unknown jongleur who was experimenting with the fatrasie.[82] Whatever the truth, it seems that Watriquet came to the fatras a little late, possibly following Raimmondin — and probably with reluctance.

As Plumley shows, Watriquet's writings do reveal a few things about him. He was a trusted royal advisor. He was proud of this rank and role, and was a snob.[83] Most of Watriquet's works are conservative, moralistic narrative poems. Uhl adds the observation that the fatras are placed last in the manuscript where they appear, which is organized chronologically.[84] The fatras may therefore have been Watriquet's last writings, and at the time of their performance for Philippe VI, in 1329 or 1330, the poet may have been entering old age. Considering these factors, Uhl wonders why Watriquet consented to collaborate with Raimmondin, who would have been viewed as his poetic and social inferior. Uhl asks: "Was he challenged by some hostile colleague, by the king himself, or one of his inner circle, to perform this disputation?"[85] There is evidence that Watriquet regretted the fatras. He complains in *Dits de la cygoigne* that his audience "enjoys and remember a hundred times better a fatras or some trifle than a story about good and honorable deeds."[86] And yet, in the manuscript, the poems are preceded by a large illumination depicting their performance: Raimmondin, Watriquet and the king, mid-debate.[87] As Plumley notes, Watriquet must have personally supervised the production of any edition of his collected works, including all major decisions about their illumination and décor.[88] If Watriquet regretted or disowned the fatras, why are they highlighted with an illumination? It could have been at the command of the manuscript's patron, against Watriquet's judgement. Or it could have been symbolic of what the fatras meant to Watriquet himself. "Curiously," Uhl wonders, "the fatras are [Watriquet's] final works: should we see in them a kind of poetic suicide?"[89]

Uhl's dramatic suggestion may not be as overdrawn as it can at first appear. In another of the manuscripts of Watriquet's collected works, an additional sequence of fatras appears to have been excised. A single, mostly scratched-out fatras sits at the head of a gap in the manuscript — all head, no body — where several pages have been amputated. The lonely, redacted, tattered fatras seems to be the only one of a second, now lost, sequence of fatras to have survived the violence of a censor.[90] To Uhl's dire question, I add: was the raging censor Watriquet himself? The answer is unknown, but the redaction speaks loudly without saying a word. As Louis Aragon once instructed, punning on the title of the Surrealists' first journal *Littérature: Lis-tes-ratures*. Read your scratches/erasures.[91]

Se vous ne faites si que brués vo père / If you do nothing but burn your father

In the critical literature on the fatrasies and the fatras, the question of the relationship of the fatrastic with the Surreal has been a flashpoint. At one turn or another, almost all commentators ask the question asked by medievalist Jean Frappier, in reading the fatrasies: "Is this Surrealism?"[92] As Frappier notes, the unlikely combination of linguistic experimentation and rigid formal constraint in the fatrasie makes the comparison attractive.[93] But, for Frappier, the fatrastic has more in common with the corny antics of humorist Pierre Dac (d. 1975) than with the Surrealist poetry of (in his example) Paul Éluard.[94] Poet and Occitan linguist Pierre Bec warned that new readers should be wary of drawing anachronistic conclusions from the poetic similarities between the fatrastic and the Surreal.[95] Uhl similarly warns that readers should not be tempted by the "Dæmon of Analogy" to identify the fatrastic with *l'écriture automatique* (automatic writing).[96] Each of these scholars is aware that many readers will make precisely this identification, just as they have since the 1920s. At first encounter, the similarities appear too obvious, too pressing. These scholars are also aware that the question has a legitimate historical basis. No amount of skepticism or fear of anachronism can negate the fact that it was Surrealists who first brought the fatrasies and fatras out of obscurity.[97]

Given the thinness of the historical evidence, the lack of direct filiation, and, on the other hand, the insistent poetic similarities, many scholars' perspectives oscillate. Early on, Porter called these poems "Surrealism of the 13th century."[98] Later refining that position, without abandoning it, he proposed that the poems actuate "a sort of unconscious and premature Surrealism."[99] Zumthor was initially insistent that the fatrasies had "nothing to do with any sort of *sur-réalisme*,"[100] and his dismissal of the comparison in "Fatrasie, fatrassiers" (1975) is often quoted as conclusive. While fatras work to liberate language from its instrumental uses, Zumthor argues, Surrealism works to uproot consciousness itself.[101] But later, tucked in an entry for the *Dictionnaire des genres et notions littéraires*, Zumthor instead makes the forbidden wager that the fatrasies form a "distant analogy with automatic writing."[102] Bec, although he ultimately rejects the comparison, admits that some of the more unnerving effects in the fatrasies compare with little before Modernism.[103]

Writers who caution against anachronism fear that such identifications will draw attention away from the poems' significance within their own terms and times, in favor of modern readers' desire to discover reflections of themselves in the past. In response, Maria Cojan-Negulescu asks, in a journal article about the Watriquet-Raimmondin fatras, whether "Beyond anachronism, is it not the business of literary creativity to inscribe itself into [historical] continuity?"[104] Her retort is instructive. It points to a key tension animating the controversy: the motivations of practicing poets are not always like those of specialist scholars. Crudely, a specialist's role is to situate a text in the context of its time, and to forensically reconstruct the conditions under which it was written and first received. Practicing poets — again, crudely — often nourish their own work through precisely the kind of irrational, intense, historically baseless identification with predecessors that a scholar cannot afford to make.

Rather than being wary of error, many celebrate the modernity of the fatrastic as an empowering discovery. Some, like poet Jean François Delisse, see in the fatrastic an unacknowledged source of practically everything modern in literature, a point of origin for a trans-historical avant-garde ranging through Rabelais, Rimbaud, and Nietzsche to Surrealism's shady parent–figure, Dada.[105] A little more circumspect, Albert-Marie Schmidt, a Renaissance scholar and one of the founders of Oulipo, nevertheless subtitled his own translations of select fatrasies and fatras "The Treasure of the Fatras: Surrealist Poems of the 13th and 14th... centuries."[106] But even for Dufournet, a respected medievalist, the fatrastic somehow "haunts" literature through the ages, right up to Dada/Surrealist poets like Jean (Hans) Arp and Benjamin Péret, secretly influencing their work.[107]

Le songe des .VII. Dormans / The dream of the Seven Sleepers

In one instance, Uhl went much further than anyone in pursuing the comparison. Where others only gesture, Uhl writes the most sustained comparison of the fatrastic with the Surrealist in all the extant scholarship. Uhl notes that the similarities he finds can be "easily verified" by simply reading some Surrealist texts alongside the fatrasies. He recommends Breton and Soupault's *Les Champs magnétiques* (1920) or Breton's *Poisson soluble* (1924). With another core Surrealist poet, Benjamin Péret, Uhl says, the "distant" analogy gets neck-breathingly close. Throughout his creative life, Péret devotedly practiced methods of "psychic automatism," the Surrealist *dorveille*. Between Péret's book *Le Grand jeu* (1928) and the *Fatrasies d'Arras*, Uhl writes, a reader can find "surprising distributional analogies" in tone, content, thematic preoccupations, and in their technical repertoires for creating the "impossible."[108]

Uhl's comparison is significant, because for many who reject such comparisons, the deciding issue is poetic form. For such critics, the fatrasies are not Surrealist because they are written with a limited set of rules, in strict meter and rhyme. Some scholars apparently take the "automatic" in "automatic writing" as an indication that all Surrealist writing is glibly formless. Michael Randall, for example, sees an actual deception at work in Bataille's translations. To Randall, Bataille's unstrict translations render the fatrasies "formless," thereby conjuring Surrealist poems where there were none.[109] Publishing the fatrasies in *La Révolution surréaliste* was part of a greater con by Breton to counterfeit "Surrealist gold."[110] Randall has a point. Breton sometimes would deem the things of the past, from whatever time or place, as belonging to a pre-history of Surrealism. And some of Bataille's translations are inexplicably incomplete, doing injury to the originals. Yet automatic writing and conventional syntax are not mutually exclusive.[111] Automatic ≠ formless. "Automatic writing" encompasses much more than the trance-based, mediumistic writing methods that produce a motile "stream of consciousness" texture. More generally, "automatic" indicates a range of procedures, including the well-known *cadavre exquis* which "automate" aspects of composition in order to bend, or rebound, the trajectories of authorial intent.[112] From my own perspective, which combines those of poet, translator, scholar and teacher, it seems clear that extremely stringent, collaboratively written fixed-forms, like the fatrasie, operate in ways comparable to Surrealist writing procedures. Each narrows the margin for the operation of authorial intent, or the expression of stylistic personality, to such a minimum that some other dis-individuated unconscious is compelled to speak instead.

Like those of the Surrealists, the fatrasiers' acephalic games of collaborative authorship functioned as a way of putting egoistic intention to sleep — or decapitating it — so that a shared linguistic consciousness could dream. This is true even when the resulting text is signed by only one author. Much of what Walter Benjamin wrote, in his retrospective tribute to the Surrealists, can be re-positioned to also address the fatrasiers: "In the world's structure, dream loosens individuality like a bad tooth."[113] Rather than individuating, the *je* who speaks in the fatrasies and fatras dissolves back into the social, into the busy, noisy world. As Jourde writes, fatrastic poetics mimic "a dream state in which ... necessity is identical with liberty."[114] "These are texts," Jourde writes, "that seem to produce themselves, in which speaker becomes one with the spoken."[115] A collaboratively authored fatrastic poem is like a semi-waking *visum* of many who, together, dream a single dream.

Atant vint je ne sai quoi / Along came I-do-not-know-what

To illustrate his discovery about Péret's fatrastic poetics, Uhl quotes one of Péret's shorter poems. He notes that whenever Péret writes in shorter forms, the resemblance of his work with the fatrastic is not only likely but "unmistakable."[116] Dufournet makes a parallel claim.[117] Each scholar chooses exactly the same Péret poem as their illustrative example, from the book *Mort aux vaches au champ d'honneur* (1922). The poem begins:

C'était un rat	It was a rat
un rat sur un bateau	a rat on a boat
C'était un rat plein de soupe	It was a rat full of soup
ou nageaient des bouteilles	in which bottles were swimming[118]

Perhaps a better way to fold historical time — to visibly close the analogical gap — would be to invite Péret himself to write a fatrasie. Fortunately, the collaborative, collage-based and mediumistic writing procedures of Surrealism provide techniques for channeling the poet, who died in 1959. Entire lines, taken verbatim from *Le Grand jeu*, can be reassembled into a plausible fatrastic *strophe*. In the doubled perspective of the medieval within the modern, the modern within the medieval, the fatrasie of Benjamin Péret speaks:

Un bras de fumée	An arm made of smoke
dans un puits glacé	in a frozen well
volait du savon	was stealing some soap
Les larmes de tes pieds	The tears of your feet
sur ton doigt séché	on your dried finger
brulaient des maisons	were burning houses
Âme faible et cul léger	Weak of soul and light of ass
je suis le cheveu de plomb	I am the follicle of lead
qui encombre la voie lactée	blocking out the Milky Way
sous les pas de l'horizon	under the horizon's footsteps
qui n'est peut-être pas né[119]	who may never have been born

Once invited into being, after I pulled together the first three lines to establish the rhyme-scheme, Péret's fatrasie came through clear and sure. In this collaboration with the deceased, a text results that is neither by Péret, by Mancini, nor by Rémi, but by all of us and none of us. What's more, the poetic séance could continue indefinitely, with success, summoning a host of other Surrealist and Dada poets. Surrealist poetry is especially accommodating to fatrasification because, even across so much historical time, their generative procedures result in such similar content and effects. It turns out, as can be seen here, that the presence or lack of rhyme and meter is not necessarily a decisive stylistic difference, in spite of Uhl's feeling that Péret's poetics would suffocate in formal spaces as tight as the fatrasie.[120] What counts more is that, in both poetics, intensification is achieved not through the metonymic transferals of allegory, but, as Benjamin wrote of Surrealist poetics, "by virtue of a dialectical optic that perceives the everyday as impenetrable, the impenetrable as everyday."[121] On the page, fatrasiers and Surrealists seem to eat from the same rat-shaped tureen.

Se ne fust une verriere / If not for a glass lantern

The question — "Surréalisme?" (Zumthor) — does not only survive in the responses of enthusiastic, non-specialist readers. It survives in the scholarship, initially because of the important role Surrealists played in popularizing the fatrasies. Today it persists because decades of debate, archival research and historicizing re-insertion of these texts into their originating context have still failed to find them any more apt comparisons — or companions — than in Modernism. Even Bec, in the very instant that he cautions against anachronistic misconstrual, admits to being gnawed with worry about the question. It's as if Bec insists "It is not true, it *must not* be true," then whispers "*but doesn't it feel true?*"[122] The fatrasies and fatras remain "poetically troubling," because even when seen in the context of medieval dream poetics and carnival culture, and even when read in dialogue with the poetic forms that paralleled or nourished them, they still stand out as anomalous.[123] They remain, as Angeli argues, "authentically eccentric," partying far from the ideological headquarters of medieval Christianity and courtly poetics. The *Fatrasies d'Arras*, even more than the fatras, represent "a magical moment of absolute non-compliance."[124]

More than most, Fritz grasps the historical verity of the link between Surrealism and the fatrastic. It was "modernity and the Surrealist experience that made possible a fresh reading of the fatrastic corpus, scorned by philology since its rediscovery in the first half of the nineteenth century."[125] Beyond any credit due to Breton's group for "rescuing" the fatrasies "from oblivion" (Uhl), and beyond modern readers' intuition that the fatrasiers prefigure later poets' "rights to rave" (Delisse), it was the socio-historical conditions that produced Dada/Surrealism that made these poems newly legible, in ways they had never previously been.

The fatrasiers were part of an elitist literary culture of Arras, not part of a thirteenth century "avant-garde."[126] Yet, as the above fatrasie by an undead Péret-Mancini-Rémi should help demonstrate, their unlikeness with Surrealist poets is more social, and contextual, than aesthetic. Culturally, they share more than seems possible. Aesthetically, the two are never far apart. Among the puys of Arras, the fatrasies developed in part, no doubt, as a way of pushing back against, and out and away from, the dominant poetics of the period — against the poetics of dream-allegory, of idealized love and of idealized violence.[127] All the same, the fatrasies were still probably a verbal amusement for virtuosic poets, poets who had become impatient with courtly poetic conventions.[128] In their modern reception, and in their contentious reception as *modern*, the fatrasies change status. The fatrasies and fatras effectively become avant-garde through their restoration by, and association with, Surrealism. Reborn into history in 1920s Paris, what were once the exploratory "antics" (Frappier) of poetic cliques could now play a role in the Surrealist revolutionary program to, in Zumthor's words, "attack the very roots of thought."[129]

En l'ombre d'une piésente / In the shade of a footpath

Such transformation-through-repetition is what art historian Peter Bürger deems a historical "return." Distinct from both "unconscious, compulsive repetition and ... conscious resumption," Bürger argues, in a situation of *return* "a later event illuminates a previous one, without there being a demonstrable continuity between them."[130] Bürger here draws on Benjamin's notion of the "constellation."[131] In these terms, the re-emergence of the fatrasies in 1926 speaks not of lineage, or of continuity, but of rifts. As Porter noted, after the fatrastic disappeared, it seems as if "impossible" poetics of *phantasmata* barely reappear in French literature until "the birth of Surrealism."[132] Benjamin and Bürger draw their maps across such gaps, in order to "root out every trace of 'development' from the image of history and to represent becoming — through the dialectical rupture between sensation and tradition — as a *constellation* in being."[133] For readers of the fatrasies and fatras after Surrealism, an image of return constellates because they recognize a defiant "poetic complicity" (Uhl) between these distant points.

Fatrasies and fatras dream. They dream events "always identical and always new,"[134] but they do not, in fact, rave. In the fatrasies and fatras, incompatible adjectives and contradictory determiners drop into the "penny slot" (Benjamin) of noun-phrases arranged in false syllogisms. Their brevity, and the predictability of the phrase-forms assemble a "superb disorder" (Porter) which turns the clean break of the end-stopped line into the edge of an abyss, out of which parade absolutely unpredictable "lexical monsters" (Angeli). These monsters work, hustle, sing, crowd, shout, bleed, eat, tumble, drown, pray, marry, fart, fight, fuck, defecate, dream and versify; they are the gushing *phantasmata* of the fatrastic. Read anew, in constellation with Surrealism, what some have called the fatrasiers' "purely linguistic exaltation" (Zumthor) functions not only as a way of weighing problems of language, but also as a means to "totally discredit reality" (Salvador Dalí). These poems sow a paranoia that consciousness itself is merely linguistic, and therefore contingent and brittle. For readers encountering the fatrasies after the historical experience of Enlightenment, democracy and Dada, the fatrasies caution that the "conceptual links which regulate thought" (Angeli) can be broken calmly, without raving.[135] They can be cut with the mindful serenity of a good pupil, one whose diabolical homework is to build self-destroying semantic automata. The poems' "quasi-scholastic" (Uhl) formality reads as evidence that the way to hell is a journey that can be made by foot, "in the shade of a footpath." The fatrastic uses the housebroken demons of conventional syntax and good grammar to undermine readers' faith in reality. In the fatrasies and fatras the very devices that emblematize, and constitute, rational order are exactly what facilitate a step-by-step, laughing descent into a bottomless absurdity. "It is not madness speaking" in these poems, as Angeli writes, but a thoughtful, rational mind who uses familiar elements to invent "unknown roles and unknown acts."[136]

---

[1] All translations from the French, except where noted, here or in the bibliography, are mine. Due to space limitations, I have not included the original passages.

[2] See Uhl 1989a, 172.

3 See Uhl 2006, 953.

4 See Uhl 1989b, 144.

5 Full 2018, 33.

6 For an overview of this tradition in medieval French poetry, see Spearing 1976 pp. 1–41.

7 Zink 1986, 106.

8 See Zink 1986, 100.

9 Ibid.

10 Ibid.

11 "DESCORT: Occitan and [Old French] lyric genre, courtly in substance, hetero-strophic in versification. The descort [...] was constructed from stanzas or versicles, each different from the others but each showing twofold (sometimes three- or four-fold) metrical and musical symmetry. The title referred to this irregularity, to the contrast between lively tunes and melancholy words, and, in one exceptional case, to the five different [languages] used in the five stanzas." (Marshall 2012, 348–369)

12 Zink 1986, 106.

13 Zink 1986, 106.

14 Zink 1986, 106.

15 Porter 1960, 106.

16 Uhl 2006, 945–6.

17 Breton 1969, 14.

18 See Uhl 2006, 945–6.

19 Dufournet 1991, 21.

20 Zumthor 1961, 16.

21 See Porter 1960, 188.

22 Qtd. in Uhl 2007a, 261.

23 Uhl 2007a, 250.

24 See Porter 1960, 18.

25 The 71 surviving fatras are by Chaillou de Pesstain (2 fatras, written circa 1317); Watriquet de Couvin (1 fatras, c. 1329); Watriquet with Raimmondin (30 fatras, c. 1330); Anonymous A (1 fatras, c. 1430); Jean Régnier (4 fatras, c. 1432); Baudet Harenc (4 fatras, c. 1432); Arnoul Gréban (6 fatras; c. 1450); Guillaume Flamang (3 fatras; c. 1482); Jean Molinet (12 fatras, c. 1465-1480); L'Infortuné (5 fatras, c. 1501); Anonymous B (2 fatras, c. 1570); Louis du Gardin (1 fatras; 1620). After the 100-year gap in the record, between Watriquet and Anonymous A, only a handful of "impossible" fatras survive: one by Anonymous A, one by Harenc, and the

four by Régnier (which, as Uhl (1999b) has shown, appear to be conscious pastiches of the *Fatrasies d'Arras* and of Watriquet's fatras).

[26] Angeli 2004, 46.

[27] Rus 2000, 274.

[28] Uhl 1999b, 53–54.

[29] Uhl 2007a, 250.

[30] Angeli 1982, 40–46.

[31] In Porter 1960, 170.

[32] Uhl 2012, 96–7.

[33] Qtd. in Uhl, 2012, 4.

[34] Trans. in Plumley 2013, 137, n37.

[35] Arnaud 1938, 18–19.

[36] *La Révolution surréaliste* no.6 is 34 pages long, with writings by Breton, Philippe Soupault, Benjamin Péret, Michel Leiris, Robert Desnos, and others.

[37] Qtd. in Uhl, 2006, 951.

[38] Qtd. in Uhl, 2006, 946 n1

[39] Rus 2005, 96.

[40] In Uhl, 2006, 954.

[41] Uhl 2012, 38.

[42] In Uhl, 1991, 31.

[43] The leading theory is that the first 6 lines of a fatrasie are formally decomposed lines of a resverie, then spliced with the basic stanza-form used in Hélinant's *Conte d'Amour*. For detailed accounts, see: Uhl 1991; Uhl 2012.

[44] There is some suspicion that the number 11 has numerological significance in the fatrasies and fatras. Even the aggregate syllable-count, 65, contributes to an architecture of 11s: $6 + 5 = 11$. Is this numerology, or parodic of numerology? While Uhl is reluctant to speculate, he does note that the number 11 symbolized transgression, excess, dissonance and sin (Uhl 2012, 50).

[45] In earlier scholarship, Rémi was referred to by his titular name "Philippe de Beaumanoir." (He was Sire/Seigneur of the seignory of Beaumanoir.) This practice contributed to uncertainty about whether the poet was the Philippe de Rémi the elder, who died in 1265, or his son Philippe de Rémi, the younger, who died in 1296. The consensus today is that the poet was the elder Rémi. His son, an important jurist, was not a poet. To avoid perpetuating the confusion, scholars increasingly refer to the poet as Rémi, and to his son as Beaumanoir. In our bibliography, where you see the name "Beaumanoir" it refers to our poet, Philippe de Rémi.

[46] Uhl 2012, 12–14.

[47] Uhl 2012, 32.

[48] The form is also known by two other names, the *oiseuse* (birdsong, twittering) and *traverse* (travesty).

[49] Uhl 1991, 31.

[50] Uhl 1989a, 170.

[51] Dufournet 1991, 22.

[52] Full 2018, 34.

[53] See Zumthor 1975, 84; Jourde, 2013, 53.

[54] Groupe μ 1990, 274.

[55] Uhl 1992, 83; Porter 1960, 14.

[56] Full 2018, 33.

[57] Uhl 1989a, 171.

[58] Angeli 1982, 118.

[59] Uhl 2012, 15.

[60] In the anonymous *Les Régles de la Seconde Rettorique*, written sometime between 1411–1432, the fatras is called the "fatras enté", with an example provided that is one of the last known "impossible" fatras, "Or gardés mieulx vos gelines / Que Rembourc ne fist son coc." See Uhl, 2012, 52–53. For the text, see Porter 1960, 160.

[61] Uhl 2012, 15. "Chaillou de Pesstain" may have been a collective pseudonym for the manuscript's contributors, rather than the name of a living individual.

[62] Plumley 2013, 129-30.

[63] See Porter 1960, 70-2.

[64] Plumley 2013, 138-9.

[65] Note that as early as 1450, "fatras" had left poetics jargon to enter the French vernacular, where it lost its association with poetry, except among poetry technicians like Harenc, Molinet and Du Gardin. By 1537 at the latest, the word had come to mean what it still means today: mess, confusion, incoherent jumble.

[66] Full 2018, 31.

[67] See Dufournet 1991, 22-23.

[68] Rus 2007/2, 193.

[69] Qtd. in Gally 1994, 71.

[70] Gally 1994, 72.

[71] See Rosenberg 1995, 495.

[72] Uhl 2008, 142.

[73] Uhl 2006, 957.

[74] Zumthor 1961, 15.

[75] Uhl 2012, 16.

[76] Uhl 2007b, 754.

[77] Trans. in Plumley 2013, 133.

[78] See Uhl 1999c, 145-154.

[79] Uhl 1991, 30.

[80] Uhl 2012, 288.

[81] Porter 1960, 92.

[82] Porter 1960, 92.

[83] Plumley 2013, 131.

[84] Uhl 2012, 288-9.

[85] Ibid.

[86] Trans. in Plumley, 2013, 132.

[87] Unfortunately the image is too degraded to reproduce here. But you can see a low-resolution scan of the illumation in the French National Library's file of the manuscript, available for free online, at: https://gallica.bnf.fr. The manuscript reference is *Paris, BNF fr. 14968*. The illustration is on page 190 of the pdf. For more discussion, see Plumley 2013, 133.

[88] Plumley 2013, 127.

[89] Uhl 2012, 36.

[90] Uhl 2012, 16.

[91] See Caws 2018, 4.

[92] Frappier 1963, 22.

[93] Frappier 1963, 21.

[94] Frappier 1963, 21.

[95] Bec 1977, 167; 182–183.

[96] Uhl 2012, 5.

[97] Fritz 2015, 98.

[98] Porter 1959, 98 n4.

[99] Porter 1960, 67.

[100] Zumthor 1972, 141.

[101] In Zumthor 1961, 14.

[102] Zumthor 1997, 303.

[103] Bec 1977, 182.

[104] Cojan-Negulescu 2004, 114.

[105] Delisse 1984, 27.

[106] Schmidt 1950–51, np.

[107] Dufournet 1991, 23.

[108] Uhl 2006, 954. Note that Uhl himself draws from yet another scholar in making this comparison, Jean-Christophe Bailly, who in his monograph on Péret brings forward the fatrasies as an important historical precedent for Péret's practice. The stanza Bailly chooses to illustrate his argument is FA 54, "Uns ours emplumés." (See Bailly, 1971, 89).

[109] Randall 1997, 46.

[110] Randall 1997, 35.

[111] Uhl 2006, 954.

[112] Benjamin 1999, 48.

[113] "In 1925 … the Surrealists played a form of Consequences. Everyone wrote a word on a sheet of paper, folding it to hide what was written before passing it to his neighbor. The first sentence obtained in this arbitrary manner was 'The exquisite [corpse] drank the new wine.' This Surrealist game in which the random procedure was a form of dream-work was often practiced in Surrealist drawing." (Passeron 1978, 259).

[114] Jourde 2013, 65.

[115] Ibid.

[116] Uhl 2006, 955–6

[117] Dufournet 1991, 22–3.

[118] Qtd. in Dufournet 1991, 23; Uhl 2006, 955–6.

[119] For readers interested in reverse-engineering the Péret fatrasie stanza, please see the Black Widow edition of *Le Grand jeu* (2011): "fumée" (68); "glacé" (70); "savon" (106); "pieds" (52); "séché" (54); "maisons" (38); "léger" (114); "plomb" (36); "lactée" (60); "l'horizon" (44); "né" (128). My only changes: "dans le puits glacé" → "dans un puits glacé"; "voleur de savon" → "volait du savon"; "brûle les maisons" → "brûlaient des maisons"; "L'âme faible la chair forte le cul léger" → "Âme faible et cul léger"; "qui encombrent la voie lactée" → "qui encombre la voie lactée."

[120] Uhl 2006, 955.

[121] Benjamin 1999, 55.

[122] Bec 1977, 182.

[123] Among the other forms usually cited as part of the literary context and/or genesis of the fatrastic are the *resverie, sottes chansons, besturnés, congés, fabliaux, jeux-partis, menteries* and *sotties*. See Uhl, 2012.

[124] Angeli 2004, 40.

[125] Fritz 2015, 98.

[126] See Uhl 2008, 142.

[127] See Frappier, 1963, 11.

[128] Porter 1960, 95.

[129] Zumthor 1961, 14.

[130] Bürger 2010, 712.

[131] Benjamin 1999, 458.

[132] Porter 1960, 106. Delisse (1984) in fact discovers a startlingly fatrasie-like poem from 1724, by the songwriter Brûle-Maison. To Delisse, this is evidence that the fatrastic was not extinguished during the blackout of neglect, but was culturally marginalized — driven underground, as it were, below the reach of the literary archive.

[133] Benjamin 1999, 845.

[134] Benjamin 1999, 854–5.

[135] Angeli 2004, 39.

[136] Ibid.

A Note on the Translations

by Ted Byrne

"...mesure des oreilles, dont le jugement est très superbe..."
– Joachim Du Bellay

Upon discovering Lambert C. Porter's 1960 edition of the fatrasies and fatras, and then marvelling at the fact that these works had never been translated,[1] we decided that we had to bring them over into English. Because of what they are, because of what they do. Because they rally the impossible, which is to say the meaning that steps outside of the binary of sense and nonsense and gives access to the real, and to the laughter that defends us from it. We came to the task as poets. We are not medievalists, specialists in Old French, or professional translators. We came as poets, bringing with us all of the license, enthusiasm, and skill that art affords us. We felt the same urgency Georges Bataille must have felt almost a century ago, when he brought them for the first time into French view.

Since these poems had not been translated into English before, we knew from the outset that we would have to take responsibility for transmitting their denotative meaning (or unmeaning) to a new audience, while at the same time capturing their poetics and their spirit. Achieving this in English, of course, involved us in all the usual problems of translation, some of which I will address in this note.

We began with Porter's text, researching each word and phrase using the splendid collection of dictionaries at the University of British Columbia. At this stage, our first draft, we did not rely on modern French translations, even where they were available. Later, we began to check our versions, where possible, against French translations, including selections, such as those by Bataille, Albert-Marie Schmidt and Jean Dufournet, as well as samples given in the critical literature. Most importantly, for the fatrasies we made use of Martijn Rus's edition, which includes modern French translations. For the whole body of work, we consulted Patrice Uhl's recent heavily annotated Old French edition. We also checked our work against Daniela Musso's Italian translation, especially for the fatras, most of which have not yet been translated into modern French.

Any errors, of course, are ours alone. We do caution the reader not to be hasty in judging our divergences as mistakes rather than deliberate choices. Although we have been meticulous, the result is not always a word-for-word translation, as might have been possible had we chosen to translate the poems into prose. But even then, our poetic impulses would have been hard to supress when confronted with these particular poems, seemingly written for the pleasure of poets. Nonetheless, we hope that a reader with sufficient French can make use of the source text to increase their pleasure in reading our translations.

It might seem odd to present the conveyance of meaning as a problem in the context of these poems, which are so unburdened by meaning. However, the problem for the translator does not lie where one might expect. These poems are not obscure, and for the most part not the least recherché. As has been well established, the grammar, the syntax and the vocabulary do not transgress the norms of the language. There are problems that relate to the state of the language and our distance from it in time. But the more significant problem lies in the extremely tight fit between the content and the form. As Jean-Marie Fritz has shown, translation of the fatrasies into modern French, or even into other romance languages, is facilitated by the straightforwardness and concreteness of the language of the poems, as well as by the abundance of rhymes in those languages, and the similarity of rhythms.[2] Translating into English does not give us such advantages.

We have not attempted a translation of the fatrasies and fatras into English metres because such an attempt, while reaching for the spirit of the poems, would inevitably damage their content, and because we agree with Henri Meschonnic that metre is a fiction imposed on rhythm.[3] The problems posed by the form pertain to both the line, with its syllable count and stresses, and to the stanzas with their rhyme scheme built around only two rhymes. Choosing a metrical scheme would be the simpler task, but finding the rhymes in English, a language not rich in rhymes, would be an insurmountable problem. The poems are virtually built around actions perpetrated by a subject on an object. It would be impossible to find rhymes without changing the repertory of characters so important to the humor.

The reasons for our decision to forego metre and rhyme can be illustrated by taking a look at the only English translations we are aware of, those few fatrasies included in the *Chatto Book of Nonsense Verse*. What follows are three lines (9–11) from the fourth stanza of Philippe de Rémi's fatrasie, first the Chatto translation, then the Old French, and then our own rendering.

A dead quail in her nest
Would have called up a tempest
Under the hat they were wearing.

Li cris d'une quaille morte
Les eüst pris a esfors
Desous un capel de fautre

the cry of a lifeless quail
would've taken them by force
underneath a felt hat

In order to get an approximate syllable count, the Chatto
translator loses the fact that it is the quail's 'cry' that performs
the action. This is a significant loss as one of the techniques
of the fatrasies is to give agency to part-objects, and in this
case a part-object that has no visible substance, and moreover
no possible existence, the quail that emits the cry being dead.
All of this, taken together, disallows the conjuring of an
image, a second important characteristic of the fatrasies.[4]
Similarly, the tempest and the nest in the Chatto translation,
which are not in the fatrasie at all, are interpolated to create
a rhyme, and completely change the action described. The
word 'wearing' is also selected in order to rhyme, imperfectly,
with five preceding words ending in -ing, one ending that is
abundant in English and thereby serves the purpose of meet-
ing the rule that there be only two rhymes. But how far could
this approach go without becoming even duller than it is in
this example? In order to achieve the rhymes, and only ap-
proximately at that, the translator has had to make changes
that distort the meaning, and even the very nature and tone
of the fatrasie. The impossible has become possible, at least
as image or metaphor.

Modern practice allows us to opt for lines of irregular
length with no regular rhymes. This is a choice dictated by
the problems just illustrated, but also a choice that helped us
make readable modern English poems of the fatrasies and fa-
tras. We have not relied on metre, but rather on rhythm, Eng-
lish rhythm — what our ears hear. As Joachim Du Bellay
famously said, condensing a passage from Cicero, "poetry is
created by the exercise of prudence and the ear's measure, of

which the judgement is most superb." The medievalist Roger Dragonetti further condenses Du Bellay into what we have taken as our rule, "le jugement de l'oreille".[5]

However, unlike the Italian and German translators, Daniela Musso and Ralph Dutli, we have chosen to approximate the syllable count. The length of the line is one important aspect of the form that can be adapted without unnecessary loss. We have allowed ourselves some latitude — a rule of plus or minus one syllable — to avoid the distortions that result from an absolute rule, and to acknowledge the fiction of number. That is, the ear does not hear the exact divisions that are implied by the notion of metre. Some one syllable words are "longer" than others, sounding nearly like two, and sometimes two syllables can sound like one when spoken. By choosing to approximate the syllable count, we have also chosen to attend to the rhythm of the line and attempt to bring it into our English prosody. We also heard Louis Zukofsky whispering in our other ear that we must avoid padding, the inclusion of an unneeded word to fill out the count.

The decision not to punctuate was an easy one to make, for the simple reason that there is no punctuation in the Old French manuscripts. Any punctuation used in the texts established by specialists in the field is an interpolation. In addition, the absence of punctuation is, by now, at least since Apollinaire, familiar to readers of modern and postmodern poetry. However, we made this choice not simply to give the poems a modern feel — they already have that — but to facilitate the play of ambiguity that pervades the fatrasies and fatras. There is a large element of ambiguity in these poems, and it is not simply an artifact of the vagaries of their transcription, or of lost cultural knowledge. Our one concession to punctuation is the use of capital letters to mark the beginning of a direct statement or reported speech, or a new thought. We have also used the ampersand for similar reasons, it being a sign which textually bridges the medieval and the modern. It is used in the medieval manuscripts, and it is used in certain modernist writings, particularly in the Poundian line, including poets such as e.e. cummings and Charles Olson, to name just a couple.

In addition to obeying a strict, fixed form, these poems, as has often been noted, do not transgress the rules of grammar and syntax. We have tried to respect grammatical constructions, except where an improvement to the English translation suggested a deviation, in verb tense for example, that did not damage the meaning of the poem. In some cases, we chose to vary the pronouns. In the fatrasies and fatras, objects, animals, places and conditions are not so much personified as given a subjectivity of their own. In the Old French these beings then have a gender, which, except in the case of animals, is most often determined by their grammatical gender. The solution when translating, with regard to objects in particular, might have been to always use the pronoun 'it'. We chose, in some instances, to use the masculine and feminine pronouns, not so much to personify as to amplify the uncanny subjectivity at play in the events portrayed.

A couple of particular constructions deserve notice. The locution *se ne fust* (if not for, be it not for), and its variants, is a construction that actually constitutes a fatrastic procedure, and we have not avoided its repetition. Similarly, a frequent construction in the fatrasies and fatras is the connection of two substantives by the preposition *de* — ".i. oés de coton" (an egg of coton) for example (FA 23). While acceptable, this construction tends to sound awkward in English and we could have easily opted for the more typical English construction, such as "a cotton egg" in the example just given, if we had not come to see this as a deliberate repetition.[6] We tended to break this self-imposed rule only where it seemed to improve the poem, for example in avoiding an unintended ambiguity, or in taking the opportunity for a rhyme, as in our translation of FA 23:

Li pez d'un suiron
En son chapperon
Voloit porter Romme
.I. oés de coton
Prist par le menton
Le cri d'un preudomme
Ja le ferist en la somme
La pensee d'un larron
Qant li pepins d'une pomme
C'est escriez a haut ton
Dont viens Ou vas
Huillecomme

The fart of a mite
in its little hat
tried to capture Rome
An egg of cotton
grabbed by the chin
a councilor's chagrin
A burglar's idea
would have struck him in the end
when the pip of an apple
cried out in falsetto
Where from Where to
Willkommen

In this case, "a councilor's chagrin" gave us a rhyme we wanted to keep, and "a burglar's idea" avoided an ambiguity we did not feel was there in the text.

With regard to lexicon, the fatrasies and fatras are, for the most part, constructed from simple, everyday words, and we've tried to conform to this by avoiding multi-syllable, latinate words. Our solutions for those few words that appear to be made up, or of unknown meaning, are addressed in the endnotes to our translation. For proper names — place names in particular — we opt for the contemporary name if it is more recognizable, although in some cases we change the name in aid of the unsense: for example, Calais rather than Wissant in FA 54, because Calais is familiar to most English readers as the point of entry to France, and thereby makes it more apparent that the feathered bear of the poem is sowing seeds on water.

In some cases, we diverge from what seems to be the most obvious definition of a word, sometimes for the rhythm, sometimes in aid of wordplay, sometimes choosing a possibility rather than a probability, sometimes choosing a connotation over a denotation, or a minority usage over a majority usage. As noted above, there is a pervasive ambiguity to these texts, syntactically but also lexically.

Fritz argues that there is no wordplay (*jeu de mots* or *calembours*) in the fatrasies. Paul Zumthor says there is no "phonic play".[7] We don't agree with these statements if they are to be taken as absolute. Wordplay is not abundant in these poems. But wordplay is part of the game, and it is a minefield for translators, since the meaning of many Old French words is simply not agreed upon, even by experts. The primary example being the word that has come to represent the genre itself, *fatrasie*. The intended meaning of some words is undecidable. Where more than one meaning seems to be implied, it becomes a matter of selection — which denotation, or connotation, makes the most sense, or nonsense. In some cases, it is a question of homonyms where one meaning alone should apply to each word. One can never assume a double meaning — in fact, they are often unlikely. In other cases, however, it's a matter of polysemy, with one meaning dominant (denotation), one subordinate (connotation). Or the meanings are meant to compete, or interfere with each other, to oscillate, creating an effect that differs from a simple pun or double meaning.

Where we find wordplay, we usually can't replicate it in English, for the same reason that we can't replicate the rhyme schemes. There are occasional puns, but most of them simply can't be translated. For example, *sacalie / sac-a-lie*, which refers to a street in Paris and to a bag of dregs (FA 26). In some cases, we have had to opt for two words where one is not possible, such as "pebble-bird" for *caillex* (pebble or quail). In other cases, we have invented double meanings where they are not clearly evident in the text, but seemed to be compatible with fatrastic procedures. For example, in the second to last line of Watriquet's third fatras (FW 3), "Car tel note me doit plaire", the word *note* has several meanings, but only one of them fits: chant, song. We took the opportunity to pun on the English word "air", which can mean both song and air, the carrier of odours, translating the line as "for such an air must please me". Our rule of thumb was to admit, but not overuse a technique where it is infrequently used in the Old French text.

In some instances where equivalent English wordplay is impossible — such as *Des Vers de la Mort* (FA 5) where *vers* means both verses and worms, or *Anguiles de terre* (FA 20), where "land eels" sounds like *Angleterre* (England) — we have provided explanations in the endnotes. In others, we can offer equivalent play, as for example in FA 15, lines 7-9, where there is no homophony in the Old French words "hanissoit" (brayed) and "orfrois" (gold braid), we have invented some in the spirit of the game:

Encontre vint Vermendois
Qui hanissoit sans alaine
Sor .i. grant cheval d'orfrois

Vermandois came to fight
& then silently brayed
on a steed of gold braid

As for "phonic play", the fatrasies and fatras are obviously shaped by their major constraint, end rhyme. But there is also notable use of internal rhymes and alliteration. Internal rhyme sometimes occurs together with alliteration. The quantity of internal rhyme is not particularly large, but it occurs often enough to indicate that, when it does happen, it is intentional. For example, in the very first stanza of Philippe de Rémi's fatrasie: Li chan d'une raine / Saine une balaine. Or, in FA 3: Vache de pourcel / Aingnel de vëel. In FW 21: C'une singesse cornue / Est abesse devenue. Alliteration is more frequent. To give just a few examples: .i. caillex i vint plorant / & une putain pucele (FA 27); Mort fussent a l'ariver / Se ne fust une faucille (FA 43); Uns saiges sans sens / Sans bouche sans dens / Le siecle mengä (FA 50). We have made similar use of both of these procedures in our translation, although, again, not necessarily where they occur in the Old French text.

A word about selection. As should be clear from the introduction, we decided to translate only the "core" works, or the main body of "impossible" fatrasies and fatras, which is to say the fatrasie of Phillipe de Rémi, the anonymous Arras fatrasies, and the fatras of Watriquet and Raimmondin. We have excluded the prototype of the fatras (Chaillou de Pesstain in the *Roman de Fauvel*), as well as all of the later "possible" fatras, because they are only of historical interest. There are a handful that are of interest for other reasons, and two or three that are, in fact, impossible and would fit our selection according to that criterion. However, they would be outliers within the terms of the selection, or at least only partially representative of the fatras written by their authors.

Once we had chosen to translate only the core works, we did not feel that we could apply any process of selection within those works, because they are of a piece, even though a few of the *Fatrasies d'Arras* and the fatras of Watriquet, if taken individually, are poor efforts, and some of them are not even fatrastic when measured against the criterion of absolute nonsense, or impossibility, established by the first *fatrasier*. And some of them simply offend our sensibilities, although not for the same reasons expressed by Watriquet's 19th century editor Auguste Scheler.[8] In our case it's not as much the bad odour of scatology as the bad odour of "medieval misogyny" that offends.[9]

The most obscene, and possibly misogynist of these poems, oddly enough, also offend the genre. In particular, they rely on the formation of a strong and continuous image or action that thereby topples over into sense, into possibility. FW 1, for example, is not fatrastic at all, nor are FW 5 and FW 10. At the same time, however, they are of interest as illustrations of the carnivalesque — the 'bas corporel' of Bakhtin[10] — and of the reverse side of courtly love (*fin' amors*) as explored by Jacques Lacan in *L'éthique de la psychanalyse* (Seminar VII) with regard to a famously obscene poem of Arnaut Daniel.[11] It could be argued, as Marie-Françoise Notz has done,[12] that the fatras entés of Watriquet draw out the hypocrisy of the so-called courtly love lyric, and mark it as misogynist in its ethic. More importantly, the most accepted definition of the pure fatrasie — as impossible, impertinent (Jourde), absolute nonsense — may simply put most of the fatrasies and fatras outside of this pernicious binary.

---

[1] With the exception of four poems that can be found in *The Chatto Book of Nonsense Poetry*.

[2] Fritz 2015.

[3] Meschonnic 1982.

[4] Jourde 2013.

[5] Du Bellay 1967; Dragonetti 1986.

[6] See Zumthor 1963, p. 162 ff.: "The two fatrasies examined contain a surprising number of groups of two substantives linked by the preposition de: the quantity of them suggests the idea that we are dealing with an actual fatrastic procedure." (my translation)

[7] "Jamais de jeu phonique," Zumthor, op. cit., p. 170.

[8] This first modern editor of Watriquet's collected works apologizes profusely for including the *fatras*, saying that he does so only to meet the imperative of completeness. He refers to the work as "a composition whose merit consists in the absence of meaning, the disjunction (*décousu*) of subjects, and the vulgarity and obscenity of its expression." Scheler 1868, my translation.

[9] R. Howard Bloch, in *Medieval Misogyny and the Invention of Western Romantic Love*, defines misogyny as "a speech act in which woman is the subject of the sentence and the predicate is a more general term." Applying this definition, he demonstrates, over some two hundred pages, that in medieval literature, from the Latin fathers to the troubadour lyric, misogyny, in both its negative and positive expression (condemnation of woman, praise of woman), is a constant.

[10] The "material bodily lower stratum" that Mikhail Bakhtin speaks of at length in Chapter 6 of *Rabelais and His World*. Bahktin makes specific reference to the fatrasie in his discussion of the *coq-à-l'âne*, beginning on p. 422.

[11] Lacan 1986, p. 191 ff. For more recent and specialized work on Arnaut Daniel's sirventes, see Agamben 1999, and Uhl 2010.

[12] Notz 1994, p. 359: "Behind the abundance of misogynistic stereotypes…and their discontinuity, lies the obsessive fear of feminine freedom, of the essential uncertitude of the amorous quest, and the anxieties of

paternal identity…In the very form of the fatras, at once broken open and closed, there can be seen a critique of the ease with which *fin' amor* strays into illusion, once again, in essence, drawing metaphoric value from 'cliché', making a poetry that would be the other side of the silence on which it is based, taking the place of the absence of which it speaks." (my translation)

Notes

The Old French text. Our Old French text was first established using Porter's 1960 edition, later checked against Rus (2005) and more recently against Uhl (2012), as well as against pdf facsimiles of the original manuscripts. Punctuation has been left out, first of all because the manuscripts have no punctuation — but also because punctuation inhibits the play of ambiguity that is such an important element of fatrastic style. With respect to the use of ampersands for *et* (and) and Roman numerals — *un* is sometimes given as *.i.*, *deus* as *.ii.*, etc. — in most instances our text conforms with the manuscripts. The commonplace word usually spelled "mout" (much, many, in great quantity) is spelled "molt" so consistently in the manuscript of the FA that we have used the latter spelling, as does Rus.

Numbering of the poems. There are two accepted ways of numbering the fatrasies. The traditional system numbers the stanzas of the *Fatrasies d'Arras* individually, 1 through 55. Uhl's new way of numbering the poems instead treats each group of 11 stanzas as 1 fatrasie, and sub-numbers each stanza. Most available editions use the older system. Uhl's 2012 edition is the first to adopt the new system. For ease of cross-reference, our numbering of the *Fatrasies d'Arras* represents both. For example, in "FA 2.8 (19)" the number in parentheses represents the older system, used in Porter's and Rus's editions, while the decimal number represents Uhl's numbering.

Rationale for the endnotes. The endnotes are mostly intended to provide insight into our decisions as translators, especially where we veer from the most obvious or most direct translations. For reasons of space, we can't annotate every such decision, but we hope that by providing enough concrete examples our style of reasoning will be intelligible. The notes also provide a small amount of historical and contextual information, especially where such information would not be easy to find online. For exhaustive historical and linguistic annotations of these poems, see Uhl's edition of the complete corpus, or Rus's edition-translation of the fatrasies.

Abbreviations Key

(FR) = Fatrasie of Philippe de Rémi
(FA) = Fatrasies of Arras
(FW) = Fatras of Watriquet and Raimmondin

*

Endnotes.

FR 1.1 "Li chan d'une raine." "Warnaviler": a farm near the seigneury of Beaumanoir, where Philippe de Rémi had his estate. Places are often protagonists in Rémi's fatrasie, so he probably means "if not for the *farm of* Warnavillers," the place itself, rather than the people who worked and lived there.

FR 1.2 "Li piés d'un sueron." "La moule …": Although scholars have been reluctant to see word-play and second-order meanings (other than certain double-entendres) in these poems, Martijn Rus provides a fascinating gloss on this unusually rich line. "Jon" can mean "wick," in an everyday setting. In carnival contexts, it can mean "bauble" or "marotte," the type of wand carried by jesters, carved into the shape of a tiny human head. A more direct translation of this line would be: "the marrow of a marotte." The "marrow" of this bauble can be understood as "the marrow of madness," or in another phrase "the pith of delirium." By choosing "jester," we hope the essence of the line is conveyed better. "Limon": usually means, as Uhl writes, "limon de charrette," the shafts used to attach a horse to a cart. However, Rus gives "lime" (the fruit) as a possible definition. "Lime" seems the better translation, given the importance of food in the fatrasies, and also the sense that intense sourness is a kind of *biting* sensation, which make the lime cohere semantically with the mention of pain and the presence of the lion earlier in the stanza.

FR 1.3 "Je vi toute mer." "& pois…": Peas and beans, like most of the foodstuffs mentioned in the fatrasies and fatras — kippered herring, peas, garlic, flans, cheese, eggs, leeks — were foods associated with Lent, and with carnival and with insanity. As Rus (2009) documents, pea mush was fed to the insane, and yet peas were also a suspected cause of madness. Jesters carried rattles made with dried peas inside. "Sur un chat…": Cats are the most common animal in the fatrasies and fatras. Dufournet (1991) thinks this may be because of the cat's association with the paranormal. Like a fatrasie, a demonic cat is a shape-shifter. Here, the cat motif is mixed with a motif from carnival culture, when social roles were ritualistically inverted; beggars were parodically crowned as kings. But as Angeli has noted, it is typical of the fatrastic that the logic of the transformation here is not, as it often was in carnival, simply polar. Mashed peas mounting a cat to become king is not a simple binary inversion of high and low social positions.

FR 1.4 "Uns grans herens sors." "Esfors": a tricky word — one of the terms that Georges Bataille tripped over in his translations. It can mean "quickly" or "right away." In context, it added martial connotations of "reinforcement" and "by force" (Greimas; Hindley). Godefroy gives both meanings, bound up together: force and speed. "Torte": can mean either "hunchback" (which is how Rus translates it) or a type of round bread loaf. Scholars are reluctant to see puns in these poems, but Zumthor (1963), curiously, insists on this one. In translating the word, we allowed ourselves "pastry." But puns work differently in the fatrasies and fatras than in other texts, because the poems give a reader no ground on which to decide on one meaning over another. Normally, a pun is additive. Consider the famous photograph by Man Ray, "Le Violon d'Ingres"; the viewer sees a woman's back that is *also a violin*. Many nouns in fatrasies have no such primary significance, given that in a fatrasie anything can do anything, and anything can happen at any turn. In this instance, "torte" is not first of all a hunchback and then *also* bread, but both and neither, in oscillation.

FR 1.5 "Li cras d'un poulet." "& une pume pourie": Uhl notes that rotten apples were among the attributes of the fool. Fools fought by throwing eggs, cheese and rotten crabapples.

FR 1.7 "Une grant vendoise." "Blé": does mean "wheat", or "field of wheat," but it also refers to any cereal crop (Hindley). The most important grains in France of the period were rye, wheat, barley, and oats. Used in brewing beer, barley is most apt here because the stanza ends with an image of universal drunkenness.

FR 1.9 "Li chiés d'une trelle." "Chaloreille": Rus and Uhl note that this is the only known occurrence of this word. Speculations about what the word could mean have included something to do with heat or heating (Hindley), a cauldron (Uhl), an unknown animal (Zumthor), a shore bird (Pérez), or a jester's cap-and-bells (Rus). Godefroy puts a question mark beside the word. Although there are few nonce words in the fatrasies and fatras, this may well be one coined by Rémi.

FR 1.11 "Gornais & Ressons." "Flaöns": flans in this context were cakes of any sort of pâté (Uhl), not the custard tarts of today. Foods of Lent, these flans were commonly made with fish or with peas.

*

FA 1.1 (1) "Jaler sans froidure." "Jaler" looks like a verb, but Godefroy gives "jaler" as a substantive noun, meaning "frost." A more direct translation of this line would be: "Frost without cold." "Dynant": a town that was known for the high quality of the copper produced there.

FA 1.2 (2) "Fourmage de laine." "Li siecles...": Uhl provides a more literal translation of this line, as "Le monde se partagea en deux" or, "The world divided into two." Our translation highlights the secondary function of the line as meta-commentary about the two-part form of the fatrasie stanza, and about the incessant conflict in the world of these poems. "Suirons" predominantly means "mite," and can be a figure for the smallest-of-all-things. Hindley, however, indicates that the meaning can expand to include other tiny bloodsucking parasites — flea, tick, bedbug — even though these bugs also had their own names. "Mui": a measurement that varied in quantity from region to region, and which indicated quite different amounts, depending on the product being measured. A mui (or "muid") of barley was a different cubic amount than a mui of salt. The mui here may represent as many as 144 bushels of grain.

FA 1.3 (3) "Uns giex de nipole." "Nipole" was a board game of some kind, possibly like backgammon or checkers (Godefroy), or possibly a non-gambling dice game (Uhl). Mentions of games in these poems have meta-poetic implications, because the fatrasies were probably written using a game-like, collaborative procedure. "Poire mole": means either "soft/rotten pear" or "quiet fart." Uhl notes that the phrase was an idiom meaning "vain promises." "Gieu de la grimole": a direct translation of this line could be "game of grimaces," but "grimole" as such is not attested outside the FA, and Godefroy has no entry for this word. If "grimole" means "grimace," the joke seems to be about a battle, or a debate, conducted solely with facial expressions.

FA 1.4 (4) "Andoille de voirre." "Juerre" and "jorroise" (FR 1.7) refers to Jouarre, in Northern France, where an important abbey was founded in seventh century. Given the current of medieval comedy about monks' giant appetites, and given that the "prune of Jouarre" gets the world drunk in FR 1.7, the implied joke seems to be that a "hanap de Juerre" (a Jouarrian tankard) contains an impossible amount of beer.

FA 1.5 (5) "Dui rat userier." "Vers de la Mort": one of the clearest literary allusions in the FA. It is also one of the rare puns to be generally accepted in the critical literature: "vers" (verse) and "vers" (worms). A direct translation would be: "Verses of the Dead," but we thought it important to bring forward the pun rather than the allusion. The line alludes to various pieces with this title, including one by the major Arras poet of the period, Adam de la Halle (d. 1287). Another was by a monk named Hélinant, in which he rails against earthly pleasures and frivolity. Yet another was by a poet named Robert le Clerc, who was close to the poetry circles of Arras that produced the fatrasies.

FA 1.6 (6) "Formaige de grue." "Grue" denotes a "crane," the bird. Rus specifies that the connotation of "grue" is "imbecile." Because cheese is associated with mental disorder, carnival and fools, it seemed important here to bring forward the connotation.

FA 1.7 (7) "En l'angle d'un con." "Crazpois": refers to fatty whale-meat, a high-calorie food of the poor which was always served with peas. The term could be translated "pois au lard" (Rus), or beans/peas with lard/fat/bacon. Cooking techniques for making "pois au lard" included boiling and baking, somewhat like the dish *cassoulet* or traditional British recipes for baked beans.

FA 1.10 (10) "Je vi une crois." "Lymeçons": although usually referring to the snail or escargot, Hindley adds that it can also mean "tortoise." Both are edible creatures that crawl slowly. "Harpë & Godiere": is thought to be fake English, a parodic stylization of an expression like "Help & God be feared."

FA 2.6 (17) "Li sons d'un cornet." "Si li ont...": One of the punishments for thieves was the mutilation or dismemberment of an ear. François Villon mentions the practice in the first and seventh of his ballads written in criminal jargon, referring to "vengendeurs des ances circuncis" or "'harvesters' [thieves] with circumcised ears." (see Sargent-Baur 1994, 300–1; 310–11)

FA 2.7 (18) "Crasses pierres moles." The manuscript is damaged, obliterating the beginnings of several lines in this stanza. "Kyrïoles": this word is not found in any other source (Uhl). It appears to be related to the Kyrie of the Ordinary mass, just as "laus" seems to be related to "laudations." Rus translates the line plausibly, but still speculatively, as: "Les laudes et les Kyries."

FA 2.10 + 2.11 (21) "Une palevole." Two fatrasie stanzas appear to have been mashed together (Porter). It also ends in a way that is uncharacteristic of the fatrasies, with the *Danse Macabre*. Uhl (1989b) established that these errors or interventions are probably what lead the scribe to repeat FA 2.9 (20) verbatim as FA 5.11b (55). The scribe seems to have realized that the distortion here compromised the fatrastic architecture of 11s, and later tried to recoup. "D'un parage lire": in the manuscript, the first letter of "parage" is damaged, although it does truly appear to be a "p." If it is "parage," it means "peer, parent, country, kinship, lineage" (Hindley). Rus omits the word from his translation.

FA 3.2 (23) "Li pez d'un suiron." "Huillecomme": appears to be parodic Dutch or parodic High German. The fatrasies and fatras include a lot of such meta-linguistic comedy, attesting to their writers' playful preoccupation with the social dimensions of poetic form and linguistic meaning. The poems are often narratively motored by speech-acts, and many of them comment, directly and indirectly, on language.

FA 3.3 (24) "Li ombres d'un oef." The scribe added two extra lines to this stanza. The second-last line has one of the only absolute nonce words in the fatrasies: "dorenlot." In this case, as Uhl points out, the line quotes Adam de la Halle's play the *Jeu de Robin et Marion*.

FA 3.4 (25) "Une viez paele." "Compissier": in one sense this term means simply "to piss all over" something. Rus, however, notes that it can mean more specifically to "piss on the buttocks" — a carnivalesque action. An alternate translation of the lines might therefore have been: "wanted to piss on / every ass in Brussels."

FA 3.5 (26) "Estranges privez." "Sacalie": Uhl sees a pun in this line, as "sac a lies" means "bag of dregs." The line is historically interesting because it refers to a specific place in Paris that is still identifiable, the lane known today as Xavier-Privas.

FA 3.6 (27) "Li piez d'une sele." "Caillex": Rus notes the unusual semantic oscillation in this word, between possible meanings, as *cailleus* (pebble) or *caillex* (a male quail). As we have in some other similar instances, Rus splits the difference by opting for "pebble" in FA 2.3 (14) and for "quail" here. To us, the oscillation in *caillex* produces a particularly surreal effect that we've tried to preserve with "pebble-bird." There are many such paradoxical or chimerical objects throughout the fatrasies, but our construction here echoes most closely the *chappe cote* (trouser-shirt) and *estaviaus bote* (sandal-boot) in FA 4.9 (41).

FA 3.7 (28) "Uns chevax de cendre." ".i. pez ce ...": "Pez" looks like the word for "fart," but Hindley also gives "pez" as "peace, reconciliation." Hence "treaty": a peace treaty. It would be unlike the fatrasies to give "fart" in two subsequent lines in variant spellings — just as many have argued, since Porter, that the double "Engleterre" in FA 2.9 (20) must be a scribal error.

FA 3.8 (29) "Uns pez a .ii. cus." "Gramaire": could be "grammar," as in a "book of grammar," consistent with the interest in language in the FA. But Uhl suggests "grimoire," a "book of magical knowledge." Uhl's reading is more consistent with what follows in the stanza, including the demonic cat and the ghost-shadow of the hound.

FA 4.1 (33) "Vache de pourcel." This stanza has only ten lines. "Qui chantoient…" alludes to the fabulous *Roman le Nouvel* (or the *Roman de Renart*, the Romance of the Fox). The poem's main character, Reynart the Fox, is a trickster figure, at home with the magical animals and weird beings of the fatrasies. Uhl (1989a) also traces the figure of the warrior-snail of the FA back to *Renart*.

FA 4.2 (34) "Uns biaus hom sans teste." "Illueques": As Uhl notes, "illueques" in a spatial sense is "here, at this place." In a temporal and/or predicative sense — which it seems to have both of the times it's used in this corpus — it functions like the modern French word "alors." Rus's translation in this instance elides the challenge by implying "so" through juxtaposition alone, whereas in his translation of FA 4.5 (37) he conveys the spatial sense of the word: "Y firent l'âne voler." "Uns biaus…": the first line is also the first line of FA 4.10 (42). Some other direct repetitions occur in the FA. "D'Acre duqu'en Occident" 2.5 (16); 2.8 (19). "Le juedi aprés souper" 2.9 (20); 1.8 (8). This is good evidence that game-like, re-combinatory, collaborative procedures were used to write the FA.

FA 4.4 (36) "A champ & a vile." "Davinés ou croiz…": eleven of the FA stanzas end with a distinct AB unrhymed couplet, introducing a shift of register, into the proverbial or (jokingly) clichéd. In these cases, the last two lines intrude with impertinent meta-commentary. The form of these stanzas could plausibly be diagrammed: a5 a5 b5 + a5 a5 b5 // b7 a7 b7 + a7 b7. Are FA stanzas 5.11 (54); 5.10 (53); 5.8 (51); 5.7 (50); 5.6 (49); 5.1 (44); 4.10 (42); 4.4 (36); 3.3 (24); 2.4 (15); 1.1 (1) key to the evolution of the fatrasie into the fatras enté?

FA 4.6 (38) "Estrons sans ordure." "Violas Bure Bure": No one is sure what this line means. Musso treats it as a nonsense refrain, like "dorenlot va dorenlot" of FA 3.3 (24). Rus puts it in quotations, as something said by the corpse of the previous line, but doesn't translate the words. On its own, "bure" could refer to coarse wool or to butter. Following Godefroy, Uhl reads "bure" as a misspelling of "hure." "Faire la hure" is to mock someone. Or it might be onomatopoeia, like the "Hure Hure" in FA 4.6 (38).

FA 4.8 (40) "Tripe de moustarde." "Chançon d'Audain": Audain, or Aude, is a secondary character in the epic *Chanson de Roland* (Song of Roland). The joke here is the pseudo-allusion to the *Song of Audain*, a poem which never existed. Villon makes a similar joke, when he bequeaths his treasured copy of the nonexistent *Roumant du Pet au Deable* (Romance of the Devil's Fart) to his stepfather. (See Sergant-Baur 1994, 112–114). In the same vein, Rabelais would eventually invent entire imaginary libraries.

FA 4.9 (41) "Saÿn de marmothe." "Marmothe": usually "marmot," but can also mean "marmoset," a type of small monkey (Greimas; Hindley). Given the recurring presence of monkeys in these poems, and in the margin-doodles of medieval manuscripts, the marmoset seems the better translation.

FA 43 (4.11) "Uns corz sainz de Cille." "Corz sainz": could be translated literally as "sacred body" or "saintly corpse," or generically as "relic." Relics can be a saint's complete skeletal remains, or they can be aptly fatrastic fragments of bodies, like the eyeballs of Saint Rosaline held in La Celle-Robaud, or the perforated skull of Saint Aubert held in the Saint-Gervais Basilica. "Byreliquoquille": looks like an elaborate compound word based on, as Uhl says, the recognized stump "bireliquoqu- ", to which the "-ille" must have been added for rhyme. The word's meaning evolves over time from simply "bamboozle" or "seduce" in the *Roman de Fauvel* to the more elaborate beguilement that "fills the mind with chimeras" (Rus) in Rabelais. Rus and Uhl take it to mean in the FA "confusion" or "entanglement." Whatever the case, it implies speech, noise, confusion and violence.

FA 5.1 (44) "Bacin chandelier." "Sommelier": A direct translation of "sommelier" would be "muleteer" or "baggage handler," the person responsible for the king's luggage (Godefroy). But the very similar word, "someillier," means "sleep." The tricky wordplay we see here is that these candlestick-bathtubs are "surrogate sleepers," who bear the burden of dreams — and perhaps also the burdens of conscience — for the king. Other references to shared dreaming are found in FA 3.1 (22) and FW 14, as well as another to a sleeping tub, FA 1.5 (5).

FA 5.4 (47) "La keue d'un pet." "Cornet": Daniela Musso translates this as "dice-cup," showing the slipperiness and the capacity of the word "cornet." More directly translated, it could be simply "horn" or "cup." Musso's suggestion fits with the motifs of performance and games in this stanza. "Boute en corroie": a finger-trapping game played with string (Uhl).

FA 5.9 (52) "Uns nis de croyere." "Jangliere": liar. In the feminine here, a slanderous or backbiting woman (Uhl). The word is connected with "jongleur," implying a rich street-life context of travelling performers and poets, who could also be con-artists, card sharps, pickpockets, and even beggars with feigned disabilities. Villon has his own mother claim to not be a "jangleresse" in her prayer to the Virgin: "Je n'en suis jangleresse." (See Sergant-Baur 1994, 112-13).

FA 5.10 (53) "Blanche robe noire." Another stanza with too many lines. At "chiens" the scribe starts a new stanza: there is a capital, and the last two lines are of 5 syllables. Uhl considers the last two lines redundant and, following Jubinal, omits them. Porter, by contrast, considered them a necessary conclusion. "Papoire": can be a type of wooden fright-mask, with a painted beard (Godefroy). Rus adds that it can also refer to much more elaborate, large-scale carnival puppets representing snakes or dragons, with moveable jaws into which people threw offerings of food.

FA 5.11b (55) "Anguiles de terre." Nearly identical to FA 2.9 (20). In the first iteration, "Engleterre" repeats. Here the scribe apparently corrects his own earlier error, giving instead: "une pierre."

*

FW 5 "Sans confort ne vivrai mie." "Douche": Hindley gives this as "clove of garlic," which often implies "thing of little value." Hence our "simple fare." If the "h" is an error, and if the word was supposed to be "douce," then the meaning is "sweet, soft, tender," and the line might have been translated: "on such sweetness for too long." "Copie": looks like a false friend, but isn't: it means "copy" (Greimas; Hindley). Uhl, however, gives the extended meaning as "use," as in "deriving (sexual) use from," or "jouissance." The word can also mean "abundance."

FW 6 "Amis puis que vous partés." "Estrons mors": If "vers" in "vers de la mort" in FA 1.5 (5) is a pun, this must also be a pun between "mors" (dead) and "mors" (bitten). Through the pun, it becomes one of several instances of coprophagia in the FW, implying an image of a tooth-marked turd, nibbled to death.

FW 7 "Puis qu'il m'estuet de ma dame partir." "Recroie" can mean "renounce one's faith" (Greimas; Hindley), but it also means to "conquer," or "force into submission." Our translation is intended to extend the fatrastic word-play on the word "croie" (cross or chalk) in the FW and FA, while knowing that "recroie" does not technically refer to crucifixion.

FW 8 "Hé gracieuse au cors gent." "Entoumi": means "numbed," or, in an extended way, "blunted." A more direct translation of the line would be: "numbed his fat belly so much." We can't see what is fatrastic about "numbed belly." Our assumption is therefore that the poet wants readers to see the belly being "blunted," in the sense that it is being made more round, fattened. "Hersent": another character from the *Roman de Renart*, an aristocrat she-wolf.

FW 9 "Quant biautez Dame a vous m'amaine." "Ochi ochi": onomatopoeic interjection, meant to sound like the song of a nightingale (Uhl). "Triquedondaine": Uhl notes that this word can mean "bauble" or, more generally, "trinket." In this context, Uhl suggests that it means something like "to learn to speak in strings of witty pleasantries."

FW 10 "Douz viaire mon cuer avez." "Pais": Musso suggests that this refers to the Kiss of Peace of medieval Catholic worship. Congregants would kiss each other, as a show of religious unity. Giving such a kiss on the buttocks, as here, is standard-practice blasphemy; the Black Mass was supposed to involve kissing the ass of Satan, or that of the Satanic priest.

FW 13 "My joy is silenced by pain." "Sambue": a special, luxury saddle for women wearing dresses, which allowed their legs to drape over one side of the horse, rather than straddling it.

FW 14 "Maugré felons mesdisans." "Clerc lisans": in the Middle Ages, reading was generally done aloud. The wealthy could hire "reading clerks" to recite from the bible or other texts.

FW 15 "En chantant me reconforte." "Pierre Remi": chief treasurer to, and a personal favorite of, King Charles IV. Pierre Rémi was arrested and hanged in 1328, right after Charles's death, when his rival Philippe VI came to power. His huge fortune was redistributed as gifts to those loyal to Phillippe VI.

FW 18 "S'ensi est que ne vous voie." "Le dons de rente": Uhl quotes Roger Dragonetti, to illustrate that, in the context of courtly love, this line must refer to something other than monetary income. Love deposits, in the heart of the patient lover, the "capital" of virtue, which later brings forms of revenue more valuable than their monetary equivalents. "Une lente": suggests a triple meaning, including "louse," and "slow-moving thing," who is "indolent." No single word in

English can do that triple-duty, so we chose to draw out the meaning across the line. The word can also mean "lentil," another food of Lent.

FW 22 "La grant biauté dame de vostre face." "Guillaume Fierebrace": an epic hero also known, confusingly, as Guillaume d'Orange — one of many Williams of Orange in history. "Fierebrace" means "proud+arm" or "proud+weapon".

FW 23 "Dame de grant biauté parfait." Someone along the way censored part of this poem. Similar censorship is seen in FW 25 and FW 26, where offending words have been scratched out of the manuscript.

FW 24 "Amis ne te desconforte." "Chien de croie" might also be a "dog made of chalk," like the monk of chalk in FA 3.11 (32). A "dog of the cross" would be a zealous attack-dog participating in the Crusades.

FW 26 "Presidentes in tronis seculi." Although the refrains of Watriquet & Raimmondin's fatras were long considered to have been borrowed from prior sources, this is one of the few refrains with a positively identified source: it comes from a motet in the same *Roman de Fauvel* codex that also contains the first fatras entés, those by Chaillou de Pesstain. All our attributions, in FW 7, FW 11, FW 15, FW 18, FW 21, are drawn from Plumley (2013). The translation of the Latin verses is also from Plumley (2013).

FW 27 "Tant est amours vertus noble & poissans." "Dist .i. sirons plus gros que li croissans": Another interpretation of this line is possible. "Croissans" means "crescent," as in the crescent moon. Godefroy adds, however, that "croissance" (referring it to the related word, "crescence") is also "feudal land rights" or "land holdings" and their fruits, in relation to the bounty of the harvest. Similarly, Hindley gives "croissance" as "increase, growth, development; produce (of land)." The FW mention property and economic relationships so often — marriage (FW 4; FW 30), harvest (FW 9), luxury (FW 11; FW 20; FW 28), the royal treasury (FW 15), debt (FW 16), payment (FW 2; FW 17), and coin (FW 18) — that the shadow meaning of this line seems to be "said a mite/ flea/tick bigger than the product of all of his land-holdings," a meaning that hides right behind the image of the moon.

FW 28 "Ma dame se j'ai pestri." "Moines bis": grey-brown monks (Uhl). Franciscan monks wore habits of this color, and their order was a powerful symbol of austerity and worldly renunciation — in contrast to the festive, even debauched, milieu for which the FW were written.

FW 29 "Amis amés de cuer d'amie." "Truie": can mean "sow," but also "siege-engine" (Greimas; Hindley), such as a battering ram, or a catapult. Given the motif of warfare in this stanza, the minority reading of "truie" takes precedence. Again, in the fatrastic alter-world, it's not one or the other but both and neither.

Works Cited and Select Bibliography

Editions and Translations

Bataille, Georges. 1926. Fatrasies. *La Révolution surréaliste* 6. 2–3.

Dutli, Ralph. 2012. *Fatrasien: absurde Poesie des Mittelalters.* Göttingen: Wallstein Verlag.

Haughton, Hugh. 1988. *The Chatto Book of Nonsense Poetry.* London: Chatto & Windus. 48–51.

Musso, Daniela. 1993. *Fatrasies: Fatrasies d'Arras, Fatrasies di Beaumanoir, Fatras di Watriquet.* Parma: Pratiche Editrice.

Pérez, Antonia Martínez. 1988. *Fatrasies, Fatras y Resveries.* Barcelona: Promociones y Publicaciones Univ.

Porter, Lambert C. 1960. *La Fatrasie et le fatras: essai sur la poésie irrationnelle en France au Moyen Âge.* Geneva: Droz.

Rus, Martijn. 2005. *Poésies du non-sens: tome I. Fatrasies d'Arras et de Beaumanoir.* Orléans (FR): Paradigme Publications Universitaires.

Schmidt, Albert-Marie. 1950–51. Le Trésor des fatras: Poèmes surréalistes du XIIIe, du XIVe et du XVe siècles. *Cahiers de la Pléiade* 11. 199–214.

Uhl, Patrice. 2012. *'Sanz rimer de aucun sens': rêveries, fatrasies, fatras entés: poèmes 'nonsensiques' des XIIIe et XIVe siècles: édition critique.* Leuven (BE): Peeters.

Manuscript Sources

Paris, BNF fr. 1588 (anc. Regius 76092) [*Fatrasie of Philippe de Rémi*] (fol. 113 v–114 v).

Paris, Bibliothèque de l'Arsenal 3114 (anc. B.L.F. 60) [*Fatrasies of Arras*] (fol. 7 v–11).

Paris, BNF fr. 14968 (anc. 63218 Suppl.) [*Fatras entés of Watriquet and Raimmondin*] (fol. 162–169).

[digital facsimiles of these are freely available through the National Library of France's website. The reproduction of the *Fatrasies d'Arras*, scanned in full colour, is especially beautiful. To see the manuscripts, visit: https://gallica.bnf.fr]

Dictionaries

Hindley, Alan et al. 2000. *Old French-English Dictionary*. Cambridge: Cambridge University Press.

Godefroy, Frédéric. 1880–1902. *Dictionnaire de l'ancienne langue française et de tous ses dialectes du IXe au XVe siècle*. Paris: Librarie des Sciences et des Arts.

Godefroy, Frédéric. 1903. *Lexique de l'ancien français*. Paris and Leipzig: Welter.

Greimas, Algirdas. 1968. *Dictionnaire de l'ancien français*. Paris: Librarie Larousse.

Kibler, William W. 1984. *An Introduction to Old French*. New York: The MLA of America.

Sainte-Palaye, Jean-Baptiste de la Curne de. 1880. *Dictionnaire historique de l'ancien langage françois*. Paris: Niort.

Tobler, Adolf and Lommatzsch, Erhard. 1925. *Tobler-Lommatzsch Altfranzösisches Wörterbuch*. Berlin: Weidmann.

Uhl, Patrice. 2012. Index des noms propres; Glossaire. '*Sanz rimer de aucun sens*': *rêveries, fatrasies, fatras entés*. Leuven: Peeters. 311–362.

Scholarship and Criticism

Agamben, Giorgio. 1999. Corn: From Anatomy to Poetics. *The End of the Poem: Studies in Poetics*. Trans. Daniel Heller-Roazen. Stanford: Stanford University Press.

Angeli, Giovanna. 1982. 'Mundus Inversus' et 'Perversus' de la fatrasie à la sottie. *Revue des Langues Romanes Montpellier*. 86.1. 117–132.

Angeli, Giovanna. 1999. Un monde à part: La fatrasie et les images dans les marges. *L'allusion dans la littérature*. Ed. Michel Murat. Paris: Presses de l'Université Paris-Sorbonne. 25–40.

Angeli, Giovanna. 2001. De la fatrasie au fatras. *Revue d'esthétique* 38. 139–146.

Angeli, Giovanna. 2004. L'incongru intolérable: de la fatrasie au fatras. *L'incongru dans la littérature et l'art: Actes du Colloque d'Azay-le-Ferron* (Mai 1999). Paris: Editions Kimé. 40–47.

Angeli, Giovanna. 2011. Les *Fatrasies d'Arras*: 'Fin' et 'commencement' d'un genre. *La moisson des lettres: L'invention littéraire autour de 1300*. Eds. Hélène Bellon-Méguelle et al. 365–376.

Arnaud, Leonard E. 1938. A *Study of French Nonsense Literature in the Middle-Ages, with Particular Reference to the Form Called 'Fatras' and to its Later Evolution*. PhD dissertation. New York University.

Bailly, Jean-Christophe. 1971. *Au-delà du langage: une étude sur Benjamin Péret*. Paris: E. Losfeld.

Bec, Pierre. 1977. *La Lyrique Française au moyen âge. Vol I: Études*. Paris: Editions A. & J. Picard.

Benjamin, Walter. 1978. Surrealism: the Last Snapshot of the European Intelligentsia. Trans. Edmond Jephcott. *New Left Review* 108. 47–56.

Benjamin, Walter. 1999. *The Arcades Project*. Trans. Howard Eiland and Kevin McLaughlin. Cambridge: Harvard University Press.

Bloch, R. Howard. 2009. *Medieval Misogyny and the Invention of Western Romantic Love*. Chicago: University of Chicago Press.

Breton, André. 1969. *Manifestoes of Surrealism*. Trans. Richard Seaver and Helen R. Lane. Ann Arbor: University of Michigan Press.

Bürger, Peter. 2010. Avant-Garde and Neo-Avant-Garde: An Attempt to Answer Certain Critics of *Theory of the Avant-Garde*. Trans. Bettina Brandt and Daniel Purdy. *New Literary History* 41.4. 695–715.

Caws, Mary Ann. 2018. Introduction: Surrealism Still. *The Milk Bowl of Feathers: Essential Surrealist Writings*. Ed. Mary Ann Caws. New York: New Directions. 1–6.

Cojan-Negulescu, Maria. 2004. Les Fatras de Watriquet: parodie ou exercice poétique? *Poésie et rhétorique du non-sens*. Eds. Sylvie Mougin and Marie-Geneviève Grossel. Reims: Presses Universitaires de Reims. 89–116.

Couvin, Watriquet de. 1868. *Dits de Watriquet de Couvin*. Ed. Auguste Scheler. Brussels: Devaux.

Dane, Joseph A. 1984. Parody and Satire in the Literature of Thirteenth-Century Arras, Part I. *Studies in Philology* 81.1. 1–27.

Dane, Joseph A. 1984. Parody and Satire in the Literature of Thirteenth-Century Arras, Part II. *Studies in Philology* 81.2. 119–144.

Delisse, Louis-François. 1984. Les Fatrasies d'Arras, Une Source médiévale de notre poésie moderne. *Nord* 3. 25–29.

Dragonetti, Roger. 1986. 'La poésie…Ceste musique naturele': Essai d'exégèse d'un passage de l'Art de Dictier d'Eustache Deschamps. *La musique et les lettres: études de littérature médiévale*. Geneva: Droz.

Du Bellay, Joachim. 1967. La défense et illustration de la langue française. *Les Regrets*. Ed. Samuel Silvestre de Sacy. Paris: Gallimard.

Dufournet, Jean. 1991. Philippe de Beaumanoir ou l'expéri-
ence de la limite: du double sens au non-sens. *Bien Dire et
Bien Aprandre* 9. 7–23.

Dutli, Ralph. 2010. Im Schlaf dichten wir den Eierkuchen aus
Nichts. *Frankfurter Allgemeine* 163. Z3.

Fritz, Jean-Marie. 2015. Traduire les fatrasies: degré zéro de
la traduction? *De l'ancien français au français moderne*. Eds.
Claudio Galderisi et al. Turnhout (BE): Brepols. 97–115.

Frappier, Jean. 1963. Aspects de l'hermétisme dans la poésie
médiévale. *Cahiers de l'AIEF* 15.1. 9–24.

Full, Bettina. 2018. Jeu de mots et forme dans la poésie médié-
vale—Guillaume IX d'Aquitaine et les *Fatrasies d'Arras*. *Jeux
de mots et créativité: Langue(s), discours et littérature*. Eds. Bet-
tina Full and Michelle Lecolle. 13–41.

Gally, Michèle. 1994. Poésie en jeu: des jeux-partis aux fa-
trasies. *Arras au Moyen Âge: Histoire et Littérature*. Eds.
Marie-Madeleine Castellani and Jean-Pierre Martin. Arras:
Artois Presses Université. 71–80.

Groupe μ. 1990. La fatrasie ou l'orchestration de l'imperti-
nence. *Rhétorique de la poésie*. Paris: Seuil. 263–280.

Jourde, Pierre. 2013. La fatrasie, un texte sans images. *Per-
spectives cavalières du Moyen-Âge à la Renaissance: Mélanges
offerts à François Bérier*. Eds. Nicolas Boulic and Pierre
Jourde. Paris: Garnier. 49–66.

Koopmans, Jelle. 1995. Rhétorique de cour et rhétorique de
ville. *Rhetoric – Rhétoriqueurs – Rederijkers*. Eds. Jelle Koop-
mans et al. Amsterdam: North Holland. 67–81.

Lacan, Jacques. 1986. *Le Séminaire livre VII: L'éthique de la
psychanalyse*. Paris: Éditions du Seuil.

Marshall, John Henry. 2012. Descort. *Princeton Encyclopedia
of Poetry and Poetics*. Eds. Roland Greene et al. Princeton:
Princeton University Press. 348–349.

Meschonnic, Henri. 1982. *Critique du rythme*. Paris: Verdier.

Molle, Jose Vincenzo. 2004. La tradition médiévale du non-sens 'illimité/absolu' (les fatrasies, les fatras et les resveries) et le théâtre du non-sens 'limité/relatif' (le *Jeu de la Feuillée* et les sotties). *Poésie et Rhétorique du non-sens*. Eds. Sylvie Mougin and Marie-Geneviève Grossel. Reims: Presses Universitaires de Reims. 37–56.

Notz, Marie-Françoise. 1994. De l'écart de langage au divertissement: la violence dans les fatrasies et les fatras. *Sénéfiance* 36. 351–361.

Nykrog, Per. 1962. Review of Porter (1960). *Zeitschrift für romanische Philologie* 78. 536–539.

Passeron, René. 1978. Cadavre Exquis. *Phaidon encyclopedia of surrealism*. Trans. John Griffiths. London: Phaidon. 259.

Péret, Benjamin. 1928. *Le Grand Jeu*. Trans. Marilyn Kallet. Boston: Black Widow Press.

Pérez, Antonia Martinez. 1987. *La poesía medieval francesa del 'non-sens': fatrasie y géneros análogos*. Murcic: Universidad de Murcia.

Plumley, Yolanda. 2013. Performing Nonsense at Court: Watriquet de Couvin's Fastras. *The Art of Grafted Song: Citation and Allusion in the Age of Machaut*. New York: Oxford University Press. 143–152.

Porter, Lambert C. 1959. La Farce et la Sotie. *Zeitschrift für romanische Philologie* 75. 89–123.

Porter, Lambert C. 1960. *La Fatrasie et le fatras: essai sur la poésie irrationnelle en France au Moyen Âge*. Geneva: Droz.

Randall, Michael. 1997. Des 'fatrasies' surréalistes? *Littérature* 108. 35–50.

Rosenberg, Samuel N. 1995. Jeu-parti. *Medieval France: an Encyclopedia*. New York: Garland. 495.

Rus, Martijn. 2000. 'Mais je ne sai que je pens': Une introduction au non-sens fatrasique. *Poétique* 123. 259–280.

Rus, Martijn. 2005. *Poésies du non-sens: tome I. Fatrasies d'Arras et de Beaumanoir.* Orléans (FR): Paradigme Publications Universitaires.

Rus, Martijn. 2007/2. Parler pour ne rien dire: le non-sens dans la resverie. *Poétique 2.* 187–197.

Rus, Martijn. 2009. Pois, fèves et folie au moyen âge. *Romanistische Zeitschrift für Literaturgeschichte 33.3.* 49–59.

Sargent-Baur, Barbara N. 1994. *François Villon: Complete Poems.* Toronto: University of Toronto Press.

Spearing, Anthony Colin. 1976. *Medieval Dream-Poetry.* New York: Cambridge University Press.

Uhl, Patrice. 1989a. Notes sur le 'lignage' du 'limeçons armés' dans les *Fatrasies d'Arras. Reinardus: Yearbook of the International Reynard Society 2.1.* 167–175.

Uhl, Patrice. 1989b. Quelle est la fonction de la 55e strophe dans le recueil des fatrasies d'Arras? *Zeitschrift Für Französische Sprache Und Literatur 99.2.* 142–153.

Uhl, Patrice. 1989c. La réputation imméritée de la troisième 'resverie' ou la tenace malchance du 'dit des traverses' (1303). *Neuphilologische Mitteilungen 90.1.* 19–33.

Uhl, Patrice. 1991. Observations sur la strophe fatrasique. *Zeitschrift für romanische Philologie 107 (1–2).* 13–46.

Uhl, Patrice. 1992. Non-sens et parodie dans la fatrasie. *Archiv fur das Studium der neueren Sprachen und Literaturen 1.* 71–97.

Uhl, Patrice. 1999a. *La constellation poétique du non-sens au Moyen Âge: Onze études sur la poésie fatrasique et ses environs.* Paris: L'Harmattan.

Uhl, Patrice. 1999b. Les Fatras de Jean Régnier: un retour aux sources de la poésie médiévale du non-sens. *La constellation poétique du non-sens au moyen âge.* Paris: L'Harmattan. 51–64.

Uhl, Patrice. 1999c. Les refrains des 'fastras' du receuil de Watriquet et Raimmondin (FW) étaient-ils chantées? *La constellation poétique du non-sens au moyen âge*. Paris: L'Harmattan. 145–154.

Uhl, Patrice. 2001. Fatras → fatrasie ou Fatrasie → fatras: un casse-tête étymologique. *Studia Neophilologica* 73.2. 211–222.

Uhl, Patrice. 2006. Fatrassiers et surréalistes: Le quiproquo sur les 'fatrasies'. *Contez me tout: Mélanges de langue et de littérature médiévales offerts à Herman Braet*. Eds. Catherine Bel et al. Louvain: Peeters. 945–959.

Uhl, Patrice. 2007a. Les Fatras 'entés' de Jean Molinet: l'aboutissement du 'processus de rectification' de la poésie du non-sens. *Jean Molinet et son temps: Actes des rencontres internationales de Dunkerque, Lille et Gand (8–10 novembre 2007)*. Turnhout (BE): Brepols. 249–261.

Uhl, Patrice. 2007b. De la structure à la performance: L'exemple des Fastras de Watriquet de Couvin et Raimmondin. *Neuphilologische Mitteilungen* 108.4. 751–762.

Uhl, Patrice. 2008. Du rebond parodique: Les pièces CLXXIV et CLXXV du Recueil général des jeux-partis français. *Cahiers de recherches médiévales et humanistes* 15. 129–143.

Uhl, Patrice. 2010. L'anti-doxa courtoise en dialogue: la contribution d'Arnaut Daniel au dossier de l'affaire Cornilh' et la tenso obscène entre Montan et la Domna. *Anti-Doxa, Paradoxes et contre-textes: Études occitanes*. Paris: L'Harmattan.

Uhl, Patrice. 2012. *'Sanz rimer de aucun sens': rêveries, fatrasies, fatras entés: poèmes 'nonsensiques' des XIIIe et XIVe siècles: édition critique*. Leuven (BE): Peeters.

Verhuyck, Paul. 1991. Fatras et Sottie. *Fifteenth Century Studies* 18. 285–299.

Visser-van Terwisga, Marijke de. 2001. La fatrasie et la poésie de non-sens. *Études Médiévales* 3. 195–201.

Zink, Michel. 1986. The Allegorical Poem as Interior Memoir. Trans. Margaret Miner and Kevin Brownlee. *Yale French Studies* 70. 100–126.

Zumthor, Paul. 1961. Fatrasie et coq-a-l'âne (de Beaumanoir à Clément Marot). *Fin du Moyen Âge et Renaissance: Mélanges de philologie française offerts à Robert Guiette.* Anvers: De Nederlandsche Boekhandel. 5–18.

Zumthor, Paul. 1972. *Essai de poétique médiévale.* Paris: Éditions du Seuil.

Zumthor, Paul. 1975. Fatrasie, fatrassiers. *Langue, Texte, Énigme.* Paris: Seuil. 68–90.

Zumthor, Paul. 1990. Fatrasie. *Encyclopaedia Universalis. Dictionnaire des genres et notions littéraires, Encyclopédie Universalis.* Paris: Albin Michel. 302–303.

Zumthor, Paul. 1997. Fatrasie. *Encyclopaedia Universalis. Dictionnaire des genres et notions littéraires.* Paris: Albin Michel. 302–303.

Zumthor, Paul et al. 1963. Essai d'analyse des procédés fatrasiques. *Romania* 84. 145–170.

Acknowledgements

Ted and Donato would like to thank the following people, for their contributions to this project along the way: Michael Barnholden, Louis Cabri, Angie Elliott, Chris Hutchinson, Am Johal, J. Kates, Matea Kulić, Danielle LaFrance, Joanna Luft, Nicole Markotić, Tiziana La Melia, Christopher Nealon, Eric Schmaltz, Leah Sharzer, Jacqueline Turner, Christopher Westcott, James Whitman.

Donato would also like to thank everyone in the English departments of the University of Windsor and Johns Hopkins University.

And of course special thanks to everyone at Black Widow Press, in particular Joe Phillips and Kerrie Kemperman.

Versions of some of our translations have been published in: *Asymptote, Columbia Journal Online, Dispatches from the Poetry Wars, Partial 'Zine, Poetry is Dead,* and *Sand.*

Ted Byrne is a poet, essayist and translator who lives in Vancouver. He was a member of the Kootenay School of Writing collective for many years. For the past decade he has been an active member the Lacan Salon. He has a Masters degree in comparative literature. His most recent book is *Duets*, a book constructed from the sonnets of Louise Labé and Guido Cavalcanti (Talonbooks, 2018). Previous books include *Aporia* (Fissure-Point Blank, 1989), *Beautiful Lies* (CUE Books, 2008), and *Sonnets: Louise Labé* (Nomados, 2011).

Donato Mancini holds a PhD from the Department of English at the University of British Columbia. His published critical writings include the monograph *You Must Work Harder to Write Poetry of Excellence* (Book*hug, 2011), a discourse-analysis of poetry book reviews; *Loitersack* (New Star, 2014), a booklength poetics in the forms of aphorism, poetry, theory and drama; and the co-edited, co-authored volume *Anamnesia: Unforgetting* (VIVO, 2013), on time in the archive of cinema. As a poet, he has published numerous books, including *Buffet World* (New Star, 2011), *Fact 'N' Value* (Fillip, 2011), *Æthel* (New Star, 2007) and *Ligatures* (New Star, 2005). *Same Diff* (Talonbooks, 2017), his most recent book, was a finalist for the 2018 Griffin Prize.

TITLES FROM BLACK WIDOW PRESS
TRANSLATION SERIES

Approximate Man and Other Writings by Tristan Tzara. Translated and edited by Mary Ann Caws.

Art Poétique by Guillevic. Translated by Maureen Smith.

The Big Game by Benjamin Péret. Translated with an introduction by Marilyn Kallet.

Boris Vian Invents Boris Vian: A Boris Vian Reader. Edited and translated by Julia Older.

Capital of Pain by Paul Eluard. Translated by Mary Ann Caws, Patricia Terry, and Nancy Kline.

Chanson Dada: Selected Poems by Tristan Tzara. Translated with an introduction and essay by Lee Harwood.

Earthlight (Clair de Terre) by André Breton. Translated by Bill Zavatsky and Zack Rogow. (New and revised edition.)

Essential Poems and Prose of Jules Laforgue. Translated and edited by Patricia Terry.

Essential Poems and Writings of Joyce Mansour: A Bilingual Anthology. Translated with an introduction by Serge Gavronsky.

Essential Poems and Writings of Robert Desnos: A Bilingual Anthology. Edited with an introduction and essay by Mary Ann Caws.

EyeSeas (Les Ziaux) by Raymond Queneau. Translated with an introduction by Daniela Hurezanu and Stephen Kessler.

Fables in a Modern Key by Pierre Coran. Translated by Norman R. Shapiro. Full-color illustrations by Olga Pastuchiv.

Fables of Town & Country by Pierre Coran. Translated by Norman R. Shapiro. Full-color illustrations by Olga Pastuchiv.

A Flea the Size of Paris: The Old French Fatrasies & Fatras. Edited and translated by Ted Byrne and Donato Mancini.

Forbidden Pleasures: New Selected Poems 1924–1949 by Luis Cernuda. Translated by Stephen Kessler.

Furor and Mystery & Other Writings by René Char. Translated by Mary Ann Caws and Nancy Kline.

The Gentle Genius of Cécile Périn: Selected Poems (1906–1956). Edited and translated by Norman R. Shapiro.

Guarding the Air: Selected Poems of Gunnar Harding. Translated and edited by Roger Greenwald.

Howls & Growls: French Poems to Bark By. Translated by Norman R. Shapiro; illustrated by Olga K. Pastuchiv.

I Have Invented Nothing: Selected Poems by Jean-Pierre Rosnay. Translated by J. Kates.

In Praise of Sleep: Selected Poems of Lucian Blaga. Translated with an introduction by Andrei Codrescu.

The Inventor of Love & Other Writings by Gherasim Luca. Translated by Julian & Laura Semilian. Introduction by Andrei Codrescu. Essay by Petre Răileanu.

Jules Supervielle: Selected Prose and Poetry. Translated by Nancy Kline & Patricia Terry.

La Fontaine's Bawdy by Jean de La Fontaine. Translated with an introduction by Norman R. Shapiro.

Last Love Poems of Paul Eluard. Translated with an introduction by Marilyn Kallet.

A Life of Poems, Poems of a Life by Anna de Noailles. Edited and translated by Norman R. Shapiro. Introduction by Catherine Perry.

Love, Poetry (L'amour la poésie) by Paul Eluard. Translated with an essay by Stuart Kendall.

Pierre Reverdy: Poems, Early to Late. Translated by Mary Ann Caws and Patricia Terry.

Poems of André Breton: A Bilingual Anthology. Translated with essays by Jean-Pierre Cauvin and Mary Ann Caws.

Poems of A.O. Barnabooth by Valery Larbaud. Translated by Ron Padgett and Bill Zavatsky.

Poems of Consummation by Vicente Aleixandre. Translated by Stephen Kessler.

Préversities: A Jacques Prévert Sampler. Translated and edited by Norman R. Shapiro.

RhymAmusings (AmuseRimes) by Pierre Coran. Translated by Norman R. Shapiro.

The Sea and Other Poems by Guillevic. Translated by Patricia Terry. Introduction by Monique Chefdor.

Through Naked Branches by Tarjei Vesaas. Translated, edited, and introduced by Roger Greenwald.

To Speak, to Tell You? Poems by Sabine Sicaud. Translated by Norman R. Shapiro. Introduction and notes by Odile Ayral-Clause.

MODERN POETRY SERIES

BARNSTONE, WILLIS.
ABC of Translation
African Bestiary (forthcoming)

BRINKS, DAVE.
The Caveat Onus
The Secret Brain: Selected Poems 1995–2012

CESEREANU, RUXANDRA.
Crusader-Woman. Translated by Adam J. Sorkin. Introduction by Andrei Codrescu.
Forgiven Submarine by Ruxandra Cesereanu and Andrei Codrescu.

ESHLEMAN, CLAYTON.
An Alchemist with One Eye on Fire
Anticline
Archaic Design
Clayton Eshleman/The Essential Poetry: 1960–2015
Grindstone of Rapport: A Clayton Eshleman Reader
Penetralia
Pollen Aria
The Price of Experience
Endure: Poems by Bei Dao. Translated by Clayton Eshleman and Lucas Klein.
Curdled Skulls: Poems of Bernard Bador. Translated by Bernard Bador with Clayton Eshleman.

JORIS, PIERRE.
Barzakh (Poems 2000–2012)
Exile Is My Trade: A Habib Tengour Reader

KALLET, MARILYN.
How Our Bodies Learned
The Love That Moves Me
Packing Light: New and Selected Poems
Disenchanted City (La ville désenchantée) by Chantal Bizzini. Translated by J. Bradford Anderson, Darren Jackson, and Marilyn Kallet.

KELLY, ROBERT.
Fire Exit
The Hexagon

KESSLER, STEPHEN.
Garage Elegies

LAVENDER, BILL.
Memory Wing

LEVINSON, HELLER.
from stone this running
LinguaQuake
Seep (forthcoming)
Tenebraed
Un-
Wrack Lariat

OLSON, JOHN.
Backscatter: New and Selected Poems
Dada Budapest
Larynx Galaxy

OSUNDARE, NIYI.
City Without People: The Katrina Poems

ROBERTSON, MEBANE.
An American Unconscious
Signal from Draco: New and Selected Poems

ROTHENBERG, JEROME.
Concealments and Caprichos
Eye of Witness: A Jerome Rothenberg Reader. Edited with commentaries by Heriberto Yepez & Jerome Rothenberg.
The President of Desolation & Other Poems

SAÏD, AMINA.
The Present Tense of the World: Poems 2000–2009. Translated with an introduction by Marilyn Hacker.

SHIVANI, ANIS.
Soraya (Sonnets)

WARD, JERRY W., JR.
Fractal Song

ANTHOLOGIES / BIOGRAPHIES

Barbaric Vast & Wild: A Gathering of Outside and Subterranean Poetry (Poems for the Millennium, vol. 5). Editors: Jerome Rothenberg and John Bloomberg-Rissman

Clayton Eshleman: The Whole Art by Stuart Kendall

Revolution of the Mind: The Life of André Breton by Mark Polizzotti

WWW.BLACKWIDOWPRESS.COM